IMPRESSIONS OF NEW YORK

Impressions of New York

Prints from the New-York Historical Society

Marilyn Symmes

PRINCETON ARCHITECTURAL PRESS, NEW YORK

IN COLLABORATION WITH
THE NEW-YORK HISTORICAL SOCIETY

PUBLISHED IN CELEBRATION OF THE SOCIETY'S 200TH ANNIVERSARY

PUBLISHED BY
PRINCETON ARCHITECTURAL PRESS
37 EAST SEVENTH STREET
NEW YORK, NEW YORK 10003

For a free catalogue of books, call 1.800.722.6657.
Visit our web site at www.papress.com.

Printed and bound in China
08 07 06 05 5 4 3 2 1 First edition

EDITING: Nancy Eklund Later
DESIGN: Deb Wood
PHOTOGRAPHY: Glenn Castellano

FRONT COVER: Currier & Ives, detail of *The Great East River Suspension Bridge Connecting the Cities of New York & Brooklyn, Showing Also the Splendid Panorama of the Bay and the Port of New York* 1885
BACK COVER: Yvonne Jacquette, detail of *New York Harbor Composite* 2003
FRONTISPIECE: Nathaniel Currier, *New York Bay from the Telegraph Station* c. 1850

LIBRARY OF CONGRESS CATALOGING-IN-PUBLICATION DATA

Symmes, Marilyn F.
 Impressions of New York : prints from the New-York Historical Society / Marilyn Symmes.— 1st ed.
     p. cm.
 Includes bibliographical references and index.
 ISBN 1–56898–492–8 (alk. paper)
 1. New York (N.Y.)—In art—Catalogs. 2. Prints—New York (State)—New York—Catalogs. 3. New-York Historical Society—Catalogs. 4. New York (N.Y.)—History. I. New-York Historical Society. II. Title.

NE954.2.S96 2004
769'.4367471'0747471—dc22
                              2004017681

CONTENTS

LITH. & PUB. BY H.R. ROBINSON. 142 NASSAU ST. NEW-YORK.

THE GOVERNMENT HOUSE.

This edifice was erected 1790, at the foot of Broad Way, facing the Bowling Green. It was originally designed for the Residence of Gen.ᵗ Washington (then President of the United States,) but, the Capitol being removed, he never occupied it,
It then became the Governors' House, and was the residence of Governors George Clinton, and John Jay. The building was subsequently used for the Custom House, from the year 1799 until 1815, when it was taken down.

It has been my genuine good fortune to have been appointed president of the New-York Historical Society in time for the publication of *Impressions of New York*. It is my fervent hope that this book, which highlights the remarkable prints from our collection of New York City views, will not only be greeted with pleasure and perhaps nostalgia, but that it also will serve to introduce readers to many of the treasures of the New-York Historical Society's Print Room.

This selection of prints, assembled by guest curator Marilyn Symmes, documents the city from its earliest times, when only clusters of low-rise buildings hugged the horizon, to the present, when a multitude of skyscrapers crowd the skyline. From historic print rarities that have survived the course of time to contemporary prints by living artists, this particular group, carefully culled from a collection of more than 175,000 prints, is brought together to celebrate the New-York Historical Society's bicentennial.

Founded in 1804 by prominent businessmen and civic leaders, this institution—the oldest museum in continuous operation in the city and the second oldest historical society in the country—took as its mission the collection and preservation of documents and artifacts pertaining to the history of New York and of the United States, then in the initial stages of nationhood. Prints entered the society's collection within its first decade and have been an integral part of its holdings ever since. Its extensive European and American graphic works range from the engraved copper plates for Johannes Stradanus's sixteenth-century *Americae*

Retectio [America rediscovered] honoring the New World explorers Christopher Columbus, Ferdinand Magellan, and Amerigo Vespucci, to John J. Audubon's celebrated double-elephant folio *Birds of America* of 1827–38 (Audubon's watercolors are also in the society's collection), to the contemporary views of the city featured in this book. Printed views of New York City and New York State comprise about one third of the entire print collection, which is also notable for its naval and maritime scenes, Civil War images, American portraits, and records of daily life. Together with the encyclopedic print collections in the New York Public Library and the Metropolitan Museum of Art—both of which are strong in New York City views—the society's repository forms part of the essential triumvirate of New York City historical prints. We prize these views as part of a vast pictorial record of this wonderful city, its people, events, and places.

I am very grateful to Ms. Symmes and to all of the staff members of the New-York Historical Society who brought this book to fruition. That it was a labor of love is clearly evident in the product. From my perspective, the book not only provides an invaluable context for understanding New York City's history and artistic culture, but it is also a treat for the eyes and for the mind. I truly hope that each reader will derive as much pleasure from *Impressions* as did those of us involved in its creation.

Louise Mirrer, President and CEO
The New-York Historical Society

THE SECOND HOME OF THE NEW-YORK HISTORICAL SOCIETY
This 1847 lithograph by W. J. Condit, made after a watercolor by Charles C. Milbourne (also in the society's collection), depicts Government House as it appeared in 1797, a decade before the New-York Historical Society took up residence there and twenty years after it was built to house the president of the United States (which it ultimately never did; the nation's capital was relocated to Philadelphia prior to the building's completion).

THE CURRENT HOME OF THE NEW-YORK
HISTORICAL SOCIETY
*This 1940 etching by Ernest D. Roth, a print-
maker noted for architectural and city views, was
commissioned by the society to celebrate the
expansion of the elegant, Classical-revival–style
building on Central Park West at 77th Street that
has been its permanent home since 1908.*

ACKNOWLEDGMENTS

I extend great gratitude to the many New-York
Historical Society colleagues who have been vitally
instrumental in the realization of this book. First and
foremost, I thank Rick Beard, former chief operating
officer, and Jan Seidler Ramirez, vice president and
museum director, for supporting this wonderful and
important project from the outset and for enthusiastically
encouraging my participation and efforts at every stage.
The continuation of this support by Louise Mirrer,
appointed in 2004 as the society's president and chief
executive officer, and of Stephanie Benjamin, the current chief operating officer, is much appreciated.

This book's success is in large part due to the con-
tributions of those who worked particularly hard during
the most crucial final phases of book preparation, and
I am most indebted to them: Sandra Markham was
remarkable in tirelessly researching obscure print subjects and printers in nineteenth-century sources and
sleuthing acquisition credit lines in society records, as
well as most capably coordinating project logistics;
Jennifer Gotwals graciously facilitated arrangements
with various artists, as well as the author's navigation
of the society's print collection; Heidi Nakashima and
Alan Balicki expertly oversaw all conservation matters
pertaining to the prints; Marybeth Kavanagh and Glenn
Castellano played a major role in arranging all the
necessary photography; and Nina Nazionale and Eric
Robinson were exceedingly helpful facilitating the
author's access to the most pertinent sources in the

society's Library. I particularly thank Valerie Komor, former head of the Department of Prints, Photographs, and Architectural Collections, for initially championing the idea to do this book based on the society's rich print holdings and for proposing me as author, as well as Holly Hinman, former assistant curator in the Print Room, for cheerfully providing my in-depth access to the print collection in the project's early stages. The project also benefited from other New-York Historical Society staff: Leslie Augenbraun, Barbara Buff, David Burnhauser, Robert Del Bagno, Andrea Forker, Kit Messick, Roberta Olson, Denny Stone, Lee Vedder, Amy Weinstein, and research intern Elizabeth Gaudino. I would also like to acknowledge the help received from Helena Zinkham's invaluable print collection research notes and former Print Room reference staff Sarah Osborne and Julie Viggiano, as well as from Print Curator Emerita Wendy Shadwell.

Many New York–area colleagues graciously provided information and access to their respective institutional resources, and I thank them most heartily: in the New York Public Library Print Room, Roberta Waddell, Margaret Glover, Nicole Simpson, and Elizabeth Wyckoff, in addition to Robert Rainwater, assistant director, Miriam and Ira D. Wallach Division of Art and curator, Spencer Collection; in the Metropolitan Museum of Art Department of Drawings and Prints, Constance McPhee and Nadine Orenstein. I am most grateful to Robert K. Newman and Michael di Cerbo, of the Old Print Shop, New York, for sharing their American print expertise as well as for kindly facilitating our contacts with many of the artists who immeasurably enriched *Impressions of New York* and the New-York Historical Society print collection with fine examples of their graphic vision. I extend major thanks to the following artists: Lou Barlow, William Behnken, Michael di Cerbo, Su-Li Hung, Yvonne Jacquette, Martin Levine, Craig McPherson, Bill Murphy, Michael Pellettieri, Alan Petrulis, Phyllis Seltzer, Richard Sloat, Emily Trueblood, Steven Walker, Art Werger, and Karen Whitman. Other graphic arts specialists who kindly provided significant assistance and insights for this project are: Sylvan Cole, Joseph Goddu, David Kiehl, Jeff Lee, Mary Ryan, Kim Schmidt, and Susan Teller. I am grateful to Andrew S. Dolkart for his invaluable architectural history expertise in relation to specific prints.

Finally, but certainly not least, I wish to acknowledge my appreciation to Nancy Eklund Later for her extraordinary editorial insight.

Marilyn Symmes
Guest Curator

Sometime around 1717, a printmaker named William Burgis gazed westward onto a magnificent view from the heights of Brooklyn and drew what he saw. Spread out before him, a crowd of barques and schooners, many flying the Union Jack, populated the river. Rowboats ferried passengers between the boats and the shore, lined with docks, fish markets, and warehouses. Beyond, a fledgling colonial settlement, with its church towers and clusters of Dutch-style stepped-gable buildings, punctuated the horizon. The artist boldly labeled the engraving of his grand prospect of England's outpost—the first panoramic print of New York City—"Ye Flourishing City." This declaration proved prophetic for what would become the resilient, thriving metropolis of today. Advantageously situated on a splendid bay where several major waterways converge, the city has been a locus of commercial enterprise from its seventeenth-century beginnings. Overtaking other American cities in size and population a century after Burgis's print was made, New York has provided a paradigm of urban growth, prosperity, and dynamism over the course of its history.

Graphic artists, as primary communicators of information since since the fifteenth century, depicted Manhattan's attributes for the rest of the world to see. Engravings, etchings, aquatints, drypoints, lithographs, woodcuts, and other printmaking techniques fixed the image of New York as it took form and evolved over time. This book presents a chronology of these impressions as windows into New York City's history. Each print provides a glimpse onto the life of the city as inflected by circumstance and shaped by individual ingenuity and ambition. Taken together, these views create a composite topography of a remarkable place and its inhabitants.

Like a series of time-lapse photographs, views of Manhattan's magnificent skyline executed by different artists in different years yet from virtually the same vantage point on the Brooklyn shore capture the eighteenth-century town as it morphs into a colossal, twentieth-century metropolis; prints such as these attempt to take in the city as a whole. Others bring into sharp focus a particular scene or singular event, or communicate a sense of place—the atmosphere of a neighborhood, or the tenor of a street. Culled from the vast collection of New York views held in the New-York Historical Society, the prints in this volume not only elucidate how and why the city evolved as it did but also reveal aspects of its distinctive character.

The first images of New Amsterdam and New York—and, indeed, of the New World—were created primarily by the Dutch and the English, who were among the region's first settlers. Early visitors from abroad, including the French naturalist Jacques-Gérard Milbert and the Swedish aristocrat Baron Axel Leonhard Klinckowström, also eagerly set down the typical and curious urban sights they saw during their visits. Confronted with a dearth of skilled printmakers and printers in the American colonies, these early New York

20, 52, 103

10, 11

3

artists sent their drawings and paintings back to Europe to be translated into prints.

By the early nineteenth century, skilled artists, printmakers, and printers from abroad began settling permanently in New York, transforming the city into an important American cultural capital and printing center. William James Bennett and Robert Havell, who originally hailed from England, became America's most celebrated aquatint print artists. By 1825, just decades after the 1790s invention of lithography in Germany, the Frenchman Anthony Imbert (c. 1794/95–1834) had settled in New York and quickly began disseminating this newest of printing technologies. He launched the city's first successful commercial lithography business with prints celebrating the city's grand public buildings and construction feats, such as the digging of the Erie Canal. The New York City lithograph printing and publishing firm Currier & Ives would emerge in the latter half of the century as America's premier view-maker. Others arrived from Germany: the skilled lithographer John Bachmann, the architect-etcher Anton Schutz, and the artist Werner Drewes, for example. Talented artists and printers from Poland, Russia, and elsewhere also enriched New York's creative output. Together, this multinational community of printmakers and printers, working in tandem with print publishers and dealers, cultivated a vast national and international market for American prints.

The most democratic of graphic media, printmaking traditionally involves creating an image on a matrix (such as a metal plate, wood block, or lithography stone),

applying ink to the matrix, and, by exerting physical pressure, transferring ink from the matrix onto paper. By repeating this process, printmakers create multiple copies of the image (called "impressions"), which can be distributed widely and inexpensively. While multiples may be printed, not every print survives from one generation to the next due to paper's inherent fragility and the medium's low perceived value relative to unique works of art. Many prints created in past centuries have either disintegrated from use or simply been discarded. Thankfully, throughout time collectors have recognized the aesthetic merits and historic significance of New York prints and the intense personal attachments they sometimes inspire and have preserved this valuable visual record for contemporary viewers to ponder and interpret for the insights they hold.

The journey along the paper trail of New York prints provides abundant opportunity to explore the city's urban landscape and natural topography, its architecture and infrastructure, its triumphs and disasters, its extraordinary moments and everyday occurrences. As material vestiges of the city's past, the cultural artifacts held at the New-York Historical Society form a cumulative cultural memory. Together with other associated objects and resources in the society's museum and library collections, they have the power to revive one's curiosity about the city and to draw one back out into the streets in search of tangible signs of its past.

The seeds of American printmaking conventions were sown in Europe in the fifteenth century, when graphic artists represented specific places and cartographers charted vast territories in an effort to increase the corpus of world knowledge. Their topographical views depicted the geographic terrain and man-made structures that formed a site's distinguishing features. For inhabitants of these regions, such pictures broadcast status of ownership or civic pride; for travelers navigating beyond their familiar surroundings—and for "armchair travelers" exploring the world from the comfort of their libraries—these prints fulfilled a need for mapping the unfamiliar.

Hartmann Schedel's 1493 *Liber Chronicarum* (known as the "Nuremberg Chronicle"), one of the earliest major achievements in printmaking, included the first panoramic city views among its 1,809 woodcuts. This pioneering encyclopedia of geography and world history illustrated such famous cities as Jerusalem, Rome, Venice, and Nuremberg. While the views of Venice and Nuremberg were somewhat factual, based as they were on first-hand descriptions, other city views were less so. As the woodcut artists had not actually seen many of the places they were called upon to represent, they repeatedly printed images of the same Germanic town, identified each time as a different city. In solving the dilemma of how to depict an unknown city, early printmakers duped their unsuspecting readers, who were often equally unfamiliar with the places illustrated. A similar situation occurred in the seventeenth century, when a map of Lisbon was relabeled New Amsterdam by its publishers, who could find no cartographers familiar with the New World.

Thus, even at the dawn of printmaking, when pictures were created as conveyers of factual information, some prints were unreliable records of the physical world. This fundamental fact complicates the task of viewers who look to pictorial artifacts for insight into the reality of appearance, as well as for an understanding of the period, culture, and creative impulses behind it. Even when printmakers were familiar with the actual subject they chose to represent, prudent looking is still necessary, as artists at times manipulated their views to underscore a print's message or to heighten its dramatic impact. In two Currier & Ives prints of the Statue of Liberty Enlightening the World, Manhattan—rather than New Jersey—appears in the background. Although misrepresenting the statue's actual siting and orientation in New York Harbor, the print aptly reinforces the city's reputation as the gateway to the Land of the Free. 71, 72

How is one to know if what is depicted is really as it was? Defining the degree of historical veracity versus artistic imagination, of fact versus fiction, is, of course, the fundamental crux of evaluating what printed pictures convey. Was the print based on direct observation or another person's eyewitness account? Did the printmaker employ artistic license to subtly alter and enhance a scene, or is the print the product of pure imagination? By comparing one print's representation to the actual subject, or to other visual and written accounts of the same subject executed in the same (or at different) times, a viewer can begin to find answers to these questions. And in these answers, which objectify an artist's subjective interpretation, clues not only to the printmaker's intent but also to the cultural context, purpose, and meaning of the print can be found.

In spite of this call for skepticism, a perusal of the vast terrain of topographical pictures reveals a long tradition of accurately representing the perceptible world in print. Indeed, many artists executed their views with the aid of various perspective or optical devices, including mirrors and the *camera lucida,* in order to achieve verisimilitude. From Jacopo Barbari's spectacular aerial view of Venice of 1500 that records every building, street, and canal on the cluster of lagoon islands, to Wenceslaus Hollar's expansive prospect of London documenting the northern bank of the River Thames before and after the calamitous destruction of much of the city by the Great Fire of 1666, meticulously detailed landscapes and city views presented an ordered and increasingly defined world. Highly portable, prints disseminated their world view at home and abroad. Colonial view-makers brought with them to America the graphic vocabulary and compositional formulas of their European antecedents, and their early vistas of New York's waterways and waterfront buildings 3, 7, 8 mimicked their works.

Probably the most dramatic and exhilarating attempt at accurately representing a scene is the aerial, or "bird's eye," view. Rendered from an elevated vantage point—from a hilltop, steeple, tower, rooftop, or, in more modern times, from a hot-air balloon or airplane—such images permit a detailed glimpse of landmarks in the 36, 50, 51, 56, 70 foreground as well as in the distance. Even today, when many people are accustomed to looking down at the city from the upper story of a skyscraper or out the window of a plane, aerial views of New York still captivate. 101, 165

At ground level, many topographers focus on the key architectural component of the cityscape—its buildings. New York City prints abound with graphic portrayals of monumental civic buildings, churches, storefronts, factories, townhouses, hotels, multistory apartments, and towering skyscrapers, as well as composite streetscapes. Before the advent of the blueprint and the computer rendering, architects and their employees explored, developed, and recorded a building's design through the media of drawing and printmaking (as well as model making). Not surprisingly, many became skilled printmakers, deftly rendering building plans, cross-sections, elevations, structural 14 systems, and construction details. Perspective drawings frequently assisted clients in better visualizing the architectural design of a building prior to its construction or by providing a record of the edifice in situ. 18

The sources of the centuries-old tradition for representing architecture in two dimensions harken back to the Renaissance and the publication of the illustrated architectural treatises of Vitruvius and Leon Battista Alberti, in 1486 and 1485, respectively. In the eighteenth century, Giovanni Battista Piranesi, the supreme architectural etcher of Rome's palazzos, churches, plazas, and ruins, transformed the *veduta* (or Italian topographical view) into grand illusionistic visions of the Eternal City for aristocratic tourists and gentlemen-scholars, as souvenirs of their Grand Tour. In the nineteenth century, the cultural capital shifted to

Paris. There, Charles Meryon executed meticulous architectural etchings of Old Paris that captured the glory of Notre Dame, Le Pont Neuf, and the Île de la Cité. The École des Beaux-Arts promoted these traditions of classical architecture and academic art to successive generations of French and foreign students. Before and even decades after the establishment of the first art academy on this side of the Atlantic in 1805, native-born artists often received their initial training from those who had studied in Europe or by consulting European prints and illustrated manuals. Alternately, they studied abroad, primarily in London, Rome, or Paris. They brought back to America not only inspiration derived from direct experience of Europe's masterpieces and time-honored art practice recorded in their sketchbooks and print purchases; they also brought with them valuable lessons that would influence the course of New York City's art, architecture, and architectural printmaking until well into the twentieth century.

One of the most prominent examples of architecture illustrated by printmakers was the New-York Crystal Palace for the Exhibition of the Industry of all Nations. Designed by Carstensen & Gildemeister, it was promoted as the city's first convention space and widely regarded as one of the architectural wonders of America. Based on the architect's drawing of the colossal iron and glass building, an official print issued by the fair's organizing board not only showcased New York's architectural prowess but also advertised the city's aspiration to become an international leader in commerce, industry, and technological innovation. Other prints were created expressly for the European market, to show off the nation's great accomplishments.

In addition to publicizing an architect's achievement, prints also frequently proclaimed the institutional pride invested in new buildings by their owners. Large lithographs were commissioned by the owners of successful factories, ironworks, and shipyards to celebrate their company's prominence in industry. Stores wishing to advertise their location commissioned architectural streetscapes that prominently featured their building. Major technological triumphs of hydraulic and structural engineering also commanded the attention of printmakers, their works providing an important corollary to architectural prints. The erection of Manhattan's first bridges connecting the city to Brooklyn and New Jersey—major engineering innovations of their day—inspired a flurry of prints. By the mid-nineteenth century, printmaking's capabilities to mass-produce large editions of affordable city views designed to reach a broad audience had made prints a popular means to satisfy a variety of entrepreneurial motives.

Starting in the 1850s, photography began to encroach on the traditional domain of the printmaker, providing monochromatic topographical images of stunning clarity and verisimilitude. Some printmakers explored the nuances of various graphic techniques that captured color, atmosphere, and dramatic light effects, as well as motion—qualities that eluded photographers of the period. The work of French impressionist and post-impressionist artists, which transfixed viewers

46

30, 45

53

23, 61

67, 109

the work of a multitude of artists in the twentieth century. During the 1910s, scores of monumental high-rise buildings were added to Manhattan's skyline, and by the late 1920s, local architects and engineers were racing to complete the tallest building in the world. In 1926 a *New York Times* writer noted,

> *The city is in upheaval. . . . In not more than half a*
> *dozen years the skyline of midtown Manhattan . . . has*
> *been lifted a hundred feet. . . . American vision,*
> *daring, restlessness, engineering skill have all been*
> *properly read into this marvelous transformation from*
> *brownstone to Babylon. . . . As for building for eternity,*
> *the need does not exist. Thirty years from now they*
> *will be tearing up the city once more.*[1]

96

with its representations of the flickering light and movement of modern city life, inspired American artists such as Childe Hassam to depict New York through new aesthetic conventions. A few architectural etchers, such as Frederick K. Detwiller and Samuel Chamberlain, extended the artistic tradition of rendering architecture with remarkable exactitude, reminiscent of the work of Piranesi and Meryon. The great nineteenth-century etcher James McNeill Whistler's lyrical prints of London and Venice profoundly influenced several New York printmakers. One important Whistler acolyte, the prolific American printmaker Joseph Pennell, began his career depicting the architectural wonders of Europe, but after 1908, he turned his attention to evoking the unprecedented, heroic scale of the skyscraper, which had just begun to transform the New York City skyline.

88, 100

81, 82

The extraordinary pace of New York's development, with its guiding tenet of "taller is better," inspired

Area artists and foreign visitors alike exalted the city's architectural panorama in prints, as seen by day or as resplendently illuminated by night. As quickly as new buildings rose up, older ones were torn down, their demise part of the city's endless and dynamic cycle of renewal that provided particularly dramatic subject matter for printmakers.

97, 103

90, 91

Since New Yorkers daily inhabit the man-made canyons formed by colossal buildings, it is hard to experience the same sense of awe engendered by the then-staggering height of the Woolworth, Chrysler, and Empire State buildings; yet many prints communicate a sense of the wonder and awe stirred by a city transformed through daring feats of construction, made possible by technical invention, new building materials, creative energy, and American capitalism. Within days of the completion of William C. McNulty's print of the Woolworth Building in 1929, its status as the tallest structure in the world was overturned, first by the Bank of Manhattan and soon after by the Chrysler Building; 114, 116 within a year, the Empire State Building—the ultimate setback skyscraper at 1,250 feet—would overtake them all and reign supreme until the 1971 completion of the first World Trade Center tower. During their lifetime (tragically cut short by the events of September 11, 2001), the twin towers inspired prints by various artists who initially depicted them as lofty beacons, alien to their Lower Manhattan setting, but later showed them as fully 143, 144 incorporated into the area's dense multilevel urban fabric.

Although the popularity of architectural prints waned in the late 1930s, partially due to the economic downturn of the Great Depression but also to the rise of commercial and documentary photography, artists continued to delineate buildings. Richard Haas was among those who revived interest in this genre during 140, 141 the 1970s. His art was also instrumental in promoting the historical preservation movement in New York and beyond.

Prior to the usurpation of their reporting role by photography, prints were used to document public celebrations, political events, and other newsworthy subjects on broadsides, in dailies, or as singly issued print souvenirs. Notable "firsts" such as the launching of the 9 steam frigate *Fulton the First*; the American debut of 40 Jenny Lind, the "Swedish Nightingale"; the animated send-off of the Twentieth U.S. Colored Infantry as it

62 embarked for Civil War duty; and the inauguration 68 of the Brooklyn Bridge all merited prints. Then as now, the curious were also eager to see pictures of sensational catastrophes, and nineteenth-century printmakers found a ready market for their unsettling pictures featuring devastating fires, building collapses, riots, and other violent occurrences.

Occasionally an eyewitness turned his hand to recording an event. The exceedingly rare print bearing the alarming headline *Terrific Explosion at the Great Fire in New York! Dreadful Loss of Life!!* documented what occurred on July 19, 1845, when five thousand bags of saltpeter exploded, sparked by a fire that ultimately destroyed entire city blocks and claimed thirty lives. As the print's accompanying text reveals, Charles P. Huestis, a fireman on the scene, felt compelled to record the harrowing events of the day, including the miraculous escape of one Francis Hart (shown in flight at upper right), who, blasted off a rooftop, survived a five-story fall with only slight injuries. Skilled commercial lithographers also depicted this explosion and its aftermath; Nathaniel Currier's image convincingly shows the 32 scene, with its human struggle and great acts of courage set against the smoke-veiled apparition of Trinity Church, but it lacks some of the urgency of the fireman's print.

In the modern era, the immediate and intense scrutiny of disasters offered by television and film has eclipsed that provided by prints. Thus, in the case of the horrific destruction of the World Trade Center and the staggering loss of life on September 11, some printmakers rejected graphic realism in favor of alternate forms

TERRIFIC EXPLOSION AT THE GREAT FIRE
IN NEW-YORK! DREADFUL LOSS OF LIFE!!
JULY 1845
*This hand-colored lithograph by Charles P.
Huestis was printed by George Snyder, New York*

*energy. Reaching such a pitch of collective effort, this energy has
become a force of nature itself. It is the poetry of Democracy, an
immense concert. This is not the Parthenon—that little temple on
a little hill. . . . [I]t is the obscure and tremendous poetry of the
modern world, and it gives you a tragic shudder, there is in it so
much of mad and willful humanity.*[2]

In a post-9/11 world, these words take on new
resonance. But of course, the true foundation of any
municipality is its constituents—the "mad and willful
humanity" who make a city bustle and thrive with
energy and enterprise. Centuries of artists and printmakers have focused on capturing the typical activities
and incidents of daily life encountered on their city's
streets, in its public spaces, and within its domestic
settings; in this, New York printmakers are no different.
While some genre scenes inventory the mundane
details of a refined or run-down neighborhood, others
explore a broad range of human behavior and customs
that takes place there, carried out by the working class
and the upper class, the industrious and those engaged
in recreation.

Most prints of New York City life feature the ordinary rather than the extraordinary: workers sort mail
and trade stocks, couples stroll, children play leap-frog,
sidewalk vendors hawk their wares, and pigs roam
freely in the street. Other prints reveal the distinctive
ethnic character of such neighborhoods as Chinatown,
Greenwich Village, and the Lower East Side. In some
prints, depictions of the city's congested streets and
subways speak to the megacity's unrelenting movement
and pervasive ultrafast pace. Typical street scenes,

80, 127

of representation. Su-Li Hung's woodcuts executed
from memory, for example, evoke the monumentality
and seeming invincibility of the twin towers, which
were to sadly become their great vulnerability.

The immensity of New York's cityscape and its
palpable lines of force and energy inspired one French
visitor to comment more than a century ago,

157

*Gigantic, colossal, enormous, daring, there are no words—words
are inadequate to this apparition, this landscape, in which the
vast river serves as frame for the display of still vaster human*

enlivened only by the chance encounters of passersby, hint at the role of contiguity and contingency in urban experience. Depictions of major crossroads, where cars and busses and swarms of pedestrians unceasingly converge and disperse, provide a visual rhythm to the pulsating heart of the city itself.

On Your Mark, Get Set, Go!, Red Grooms's exuberant print of runners crossing the Verrazano-Narrows Bridge, ostensibly records the start of the 2002 New York City Marathon. With his characteristic verve and humor, eschewing representational exactitude, the artist honors individual achievement as much as the city's much-beloved annual event. The American flag waves proudly overhead, an oblique but poignant nod to the cataclysmic events of a year earlier and to New York's—and indeed, the nation's—return to strength. Although it is a challenge to single out any one print that could be said to engender the essence of this great cosmopolitan capital, which has inspired so many glorious expressions in art, music, and poetry, this image is a prime contender. It evokes the dynamic collective spirit that has dominated New York life and that continues to propel "ye flourishing city" forward into the new millennium.

Today, New York City possesses the country's largest and most active concentration of artists, printers, print publishers, dealers, and institutional and private print collectors in the country. Add to this a sizable number of print scholars and print lovers, and the result is a thriving printmaking and print-viewing community. As New York's horizons expand both literally and metaphorically, a new generation of artists is fast at work pushing the graphic impulse to record their impressions of this city in new and daring ways. Following on what is now more than a two hundred-year-old tradition of rendering views of New York, they will surely lead us to bold new frontiers of expression, interpretation, and perception.

NOTES

1. "Builders of a New City," *The New York Times*, October 26, 1926.
2. Paul Bourget, *Outre-Mer: Impressions of America* (New York: C. Scribner's Sons, 1895), quoted in Ric Burns and James Sanders, with Lisa Ades, *New York, An Illustrated History* (New York: Alfred A. Knopf, 2003), 219.

CATALOGUE

I.

N. Amsterdam, ou N Iork in Ameriq.

c. 1700

Pieter Mortier (active in Amsterdam c. 1685–1711), publisher
Colored engraving

This charming print, issued by Pieter Mortier around 1700, is one of the earliest historic glimpses of New Amsterdam. Based on Carolus Allardt's previously published view (known as the "Restitutio View"), executed to mark the settlement's 1673 recapture by the Dutch from the British, it depicts the colonial community as it appeared almost thirty years before. A customary practice of seventeenth-century cartography, large printed maps were often surrounded by inset images illustrating key sites on the map; it was one of these inset images of America's important Dutch colony that Mortier selected for reengraving and republication.

While Mortier was a fairly well-known map and print publisher in his day, the identities of the print's engraver and of the artist who created the related drawing (also in the New-York Historical Society's collection) have thus far eluded scholars. Publishers rarely did the artistic work themselves, but they were eager to provide collectors with maps and images of the New World as proof of new settlements established by the most adventurous and enterprising of their European contemporaries.

Although eighteenth-century viewers might not have been able to identify the locale depicted in the print, they would have recognized the figures in the foreground as personifications of the Americas. Precursors of the now-familiar national symbols of Lady Liberty and Uncle Sam, an idealized Indian or group of Indians (usually dark-skinned women adorned with exotic feathers or tobacco leaves, surrounded by tropical vegetation) signified the American continents, just as other allegorical figures resembling native inhabitants represented Asia, Africa, and Europe. A tantalizing window onto Manhattan history combined with traditional European iconography, this rare print of early New York is a fine example of how a vestige of the past can resonate with a variety of cultural associations.

N: AMSTERDAM, ou N: IORK.
in Ameriq: 1

P. Mortier, cum Privil:

2.

Nowel Amsterdam en L'Amérique

1672

Gérard Jollain (French, active c. 1660–1683)
or François Jollain (French, 1641–1704)
Hand-colored etching and engraving, with inscription in Latin and French

Seventeenth-century print publishers were eager to satisfy European curiosity about the New World. Since few people had visited far-away North America, map collectors were unlikely to refute the authenticity of a print's depiction of a distant settlement. The inscription on this print declares,

> *New Amsterdam is a city built by the Dutch in New Holland in America, between Virginia and New England: it is celebrated for its great size, commerce, large number of inhabitants, the length and bounty of its Port, the beautiful structure of its Churches and superb buildings, and for its advantageously accessible location, that the Dutch certainly did not dishonor Amsterdam by giving its name to the [new] city.*

In fact, by 1672 (the date of this print), New Amsterdam had already been taken over by the British and renamed New York.

More interestingly, this New York view—seen from what is now New Jersey across the "Mer du Nort" (that is, the Hudson River)—is a fictitious one, based on a map of Lisbon. The Paris engraver and print publisher Gérard Jollain and his son François, who specialized in religious prints, portraits, and the recycling of old maps, did little to alter an earlier bird's-eye view of an Old World city before relabeling it as a New World colony. Today this exceedingly rare print is regarded as the most important early fictitious view of New York.

24

3. (FOLDOUT)

A South Prospect of Ye Flourishing City of New York in the Province of New York in America [called "The Burgis View"]

1717

John Harris (English, active 1685–1739) after William Burgis
(English, active in the American colonies 1716–after 1731)
Engraving from four plates on four sheets (lacking bottom margin),
issued c. 1719–21

4. (RIGHT)

A South Prospect of Ye Flourishing City of New York in the Province of New York in America

[called "The Bakewell View," showing the city as it appeared in 1717]

John Harris (English, active 1685–1739) after William Burgis (English,
active in the American colonies 1716–after 1731)
Engraving from four plates on four sheets, second state,
printed and sold by Thomas Bakewell, London, March 25, 1746

As the earliest panoramic view of the East River and New York City, this extraordinary, large-scale print is acclaimed as an important topographic record of the city decades before the American Revolution. From a site now known as Brooklyn Heights, William Burgis rendered the thriving colonial city, by this time the third largest in the colonies. He would subsequently make similarly sweeping vistas of Boston, Charleston, and Philadelphia.

Burgis sent his drawing of New York to London to be translated into print by the noted professional engraver John Harris. To execute the image, Harris had to use four plates, which were then printed onto four sheets of paper joined together, since at this date it was still impossible to make a single plate or sheet of paper of this enormous size. In its day, this over-six–foot–long view was a remarkable printmaking and topographical achievement.

Burgis's initial dedication (sadly trimmed in the society's impression) read, "His Excellency Robert Hunter Esqr. Captain General and Governour in Chief of the Provinces of New York, New Jersey and Territories depending thereon in America and Vice Admirall [sic] of the Same." The inclusion of a profusion of trade and royal navy ships possibly alluded to the festivities celebrating King George I's birthday in spring 1717, which may have provided the occasion for this picture. By July 13, 1719 Governor-General Hunter turned over New York's government to Peter Schuyler and New Jersey's government to Chief Justice Lewis Morris.

5.
View of Fort George, New York, from the West

1730–31

Attributed to William Burgis
(English, active in the American colonies 1716–after 1731)
Hand-colored mezzotint

This perhaps unique impression is one of the earliest recorded views of Lower Manhattan from the west. In 1626, the Dutch had established the first fort in the area (at what is today the foot of Broadway); when the British took over Manhattan in 1665, they took over the fort and subsequently renamed it Fort George. Made more prominent by the hand-coloring, the British flag flies over the fort as well as from the mast of a nearby man-of-war in the harbor to signal British dominance over land and sea in its North American colony.

This print is also the first mezzotint of the city. The tonal printmaking process invented in Germany in 1642 became popular among Dutch and English artists in the eighteenth century because of its ability to modulate dark and light areas into representational records of topography or likeness. English printmakers, who began to specialize in mezzotint to reproduce paintings, introduced technical improvements early in the century that resulted in such mastery that the medium came to be known as the "English manner."

Documentation places William Burgis in Boston prior to September 1730. There he would have undoubtedly encountered the work of Peter Pelham, the noted English mezzotint engraver who was the first to establish this profession in America after his own arrival in Boston in 1727. Although previously Burgis had sent his drawings to London to be translated onto plates to be printed, he was perhaps inspired by Pelham's work to become among the first in America to try his hand at the medium.

This print depicting British military might in the "English manner" was intended to distinguish the artist to Governor John Montgomerie, who was appointed by King George II to govern the province of New York in 1728 and is the dedicatee of this print. The governor died in 1731 (in a small pox epidemic that killed about five hundred colonists); since the print's dedication would not have been included subsequent to the governor's passing, the date of Burgis's work can be pinpointed to 1730–31.

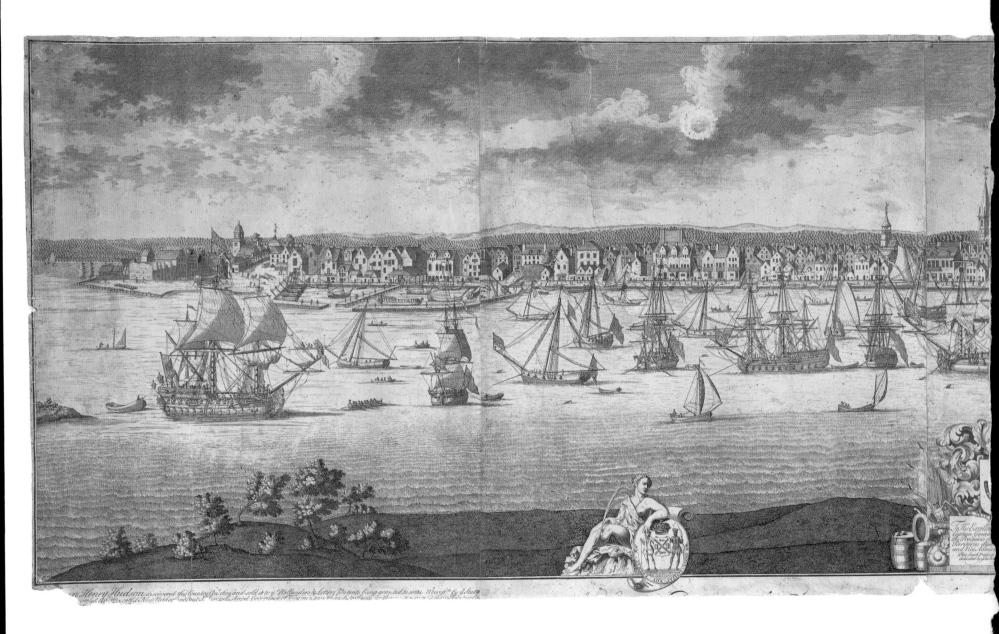

Captn Henry Hudson discovered this Country Ano 1609 and sold it to ye Hollanders & Letters Patents being granted to some Merchts by ye States
called ye ... call'd New Yorker ... out ... Generall Government of ...

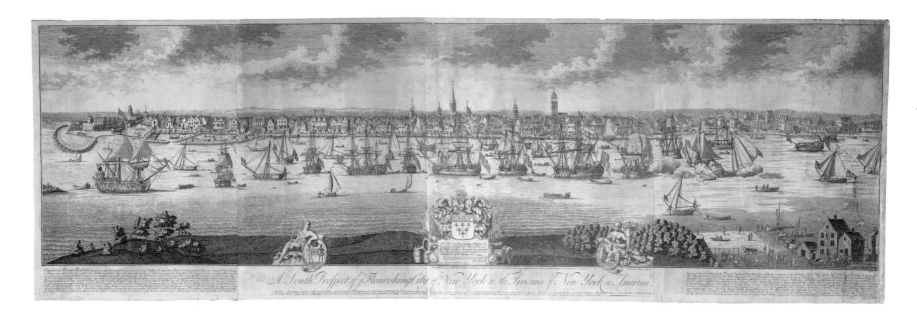

A South Prospect of ye Flourishing City of New York in the Province of New York in America.

After Harris's death, the series of four plates depicting Burgis's scene were acquired by Thomas Bakewell, who reissued the panoramic print in 1746 with several changes—notably, the addition of a few buildings and a new dedication to George Clinton, who governed New York and its territories from 1743 to 1753. This edition became known as "the Bakewell View." It is fortunate that the New-York Historical Society has both editions of this spectacular eighteenth-century city view, which survives in only a few known impressions.

Some of the landmarks visible in both the Burgis and Bakewell editions include a rebuilt Fort Amsterdam (far left), "the Lower Market" (Coenties Market or Fish Market, near left), "the English Church" (Trinity Church, center), and the "Ferry House on the Long Island side" (lower right foreground). Filled with a variety of building details, this vista provides the most accurate visual documentation of the city's skyline at this time.

To His Excellency *IOHN* MONTGOMERIE Esq.ʳ
Cap.ᵗ Gene.ˡ & Gov.ᵗ in Chief of his Maj.ᵗˢ Provinces of New York New Jersey, & Territories depending thereon, & Vice Admiral of the
Same &c. This View of Fort George is Most humbly Dedic.ᵈ by his Excellency Most humble & Most Obed.ᵗ Ser.ᵗ W.ᵐ Burgis

6.

A View of Fort George with the City of New York from the Southwest

[called "The Carwitham View of New York"]

John Carwitham (English, active c. 1723–1741) after William Burgis (?)
(English, active in the American colonies 1716–after 1731)
Hand-colored engraving, printed for Carington Bowles Map & Printseller,
at No. 69 in St. Paul's Church Yard, London; published c. 1764

The "Carwitham View of New York" was regarded as the most important early view of the city from the Hudson River (from a vantage point southwest of Manhattan) prior to the 1948 discovery of Burgis's *View of Fort George* (plate 5). A comparison of the two prints reveals that the right half of the Carwitham view corresponds closely to Burgis's earlier mezzotint.

This print provides a rare glimpse of the city beyond the fort walls as it appeared around 1731 to 1736 (this impression was published decades later). Prominent buildings include (from left to right) Trinity Church, the Lutheran Church, the New Dutch Church, the French Eglise du Saint Esprit, City Hall, the Old Dutch Church on Garden Street, the Secretary's Office, and the church in the fort. The dating of this view is based on the fact that the New (later called Middle) Dutch Church was completed in 1731, and the roof of Trinity Church is shown prior to its 1736 renovation.

A View of FORT GEORGE *with the* CITY *of* NEW YORK *from the S.W.*

Printed for Carington Bowles Map & Printseller, at N.º 69 in S.ᵗ Pauls Church Yard, London.

I. Carwitham *Sculp.*

7. (BOTTOM)

View of the City of New-York taken from Long Island

1796

Charles-Balthazar-Julien Févret de Saint-Mémin
(French, 1770–1852; active in U.S. 1793–1814)
Hand-colored etching, first state

Saint-Mémin, who was celebrated for his realistic profile portrait drawings and engravings of distinguished Americans, executed with skillful precision this panorama of the New York waterfront as it appeared at the end of the eighteenth century. The number of ships on the East River and of buildings along its shores attest to the city's prosperity as a burgeoning seaport. Although the densely packed buildings are minute in scale, many are identifiable under magnification. Beyond the picturesque foreground, several church steeples dot the skyline; until the much later appearance of high-rise buildings, these skyward-reaching structures were the tallest landmarks in the urban landscape.

8. (TOP)

A View of the City of New-York from Brooklyn Heights in 1798 by Monsieur C. B. Julien de Saint-Mémin with a Pantograph invented by Himself

After Charles-Balthazar-Julien-Févret de Saint-Mémin
(French, 1770–1852; active in U.S. 1793–1814)
Engraving (on three sheets), published by Matthew Dripps c. 1850 from an original drawing in the possession of J. C. Brevoort Esq. of Brooklyn

Executed more than fifty years after Saint-Mémin's view (plate 7) was made (and most likely in 1796 rather than 1798, as cited in the print's title), this print is one of the most accurate late eighteenth-century records of New York City between the southern tip of the island and the area now anchoring the Brooklyn Bridge. Government House, Trinity Church, the post office, St. Paul's Chapel, the jail, and New York Hospital are all clearly visible in this enlargement based upon Saint-Mémin's earlier view.

View of the City of New York taken from Long Island 1766

9.

Launch of the Steam Frigate Fulton the First *at New York 29th October 1814*

John James Barralet (Irish, c. 1747–1815; active in U.S. after 1795)
after a sketch by William H. (?) Morgan taken on the spot
Engraving, published by Benjamin Tanner, Philadelphia, March 27, 1815

This print, probably a memorial tribute as well as a document of a major historical event, was issued a little over a month after the death of Robert Fulton, the English-born painter-turned-engineer and steamboat inventor. Shortly after his arrival in New York City in 1806, Fulton developed the first commercially successful steam-powered paddleboat to ferry passengers between Manhattan and Albany on the Hudson River. During the War of 1812, Fulton was commissioned to apply his expertise to naval defense, as New Yorkers believed their harbor to be inadequately protected. He designed the 150-foot-long steam frigate depicted in this print as a floating fort, originally named *Demologos* ("voice of the people") and later known as *Fulton the First*. Congress authorized its construction in March 1814 at an estimated cost of $320,000. Seven months later, the frigate's maiden launch was witnessed by approximately twenty thousand cheering onlookers, according to newspaper reports. This rare engraving vividly complements contemporary written accounts.

As peace was declared between the United States and Great Britain in late December 1814, Fulton's frigate never saw action. Instead, it was berthed at Brooklyn Navy Yard until its disastrous destruction in 1829, the result of an accidental explosion.

LAUNCH OF THE STEAM FRIGATE FULTON the FIRST, AT NEW YORK, 29.TH OCT.^R 1814.

150 feet long and 58 feet wide, will mount 30 long 32 pounders, and 2 100 pounders.(Columbiards)

10.

Interior of New-York,
Provost Street and Chapel

1816–23

Louis-Jules-Frédéric Villeneuve (French, 1796–1842) after Jacques-Gérard Milbert (French, 1766–1840; visited North America 1815–1823), with figures by Victor Adam (French, 1801–1866)
Lithograph, from *Itinéraire pittoresque du fleuve Hudson et des parties latérales. L'Amérique du Nord. D'après les dessins originaux pris sur les lieux par J. Milbert,* published by Henry Gaugain et Cie, Paris, 1826

From 1815 to 1823, the French naturalist, geographer, and engineer Jacques-Gérard Milbert traveled along the Hudson River and elsewhere within the Northeast to scientifically observe, document, and collect specimens of native wildlife and vegetation. Many of the animals, insects, birds, plants, and minerals he gathered became part of the Muséum National d'Histoire Naturelle in Paris. A skilled artist, Milbert drew numerous pictures during his journey, noting the interesting topography and sights he encountered. Upon his return to Paris, he arranged to have fifty-four of the drawings executed as lithographs. The group comprises an extraordinary pictorial record of the northeastern United States. Since the printmaking technique of lithography was only invented in 1798 (in Munich), Milbert's series is also noteworthy as a rare, early example of the medium.

The artist's writings indicate that he was not particularly captivated by New York's buildings, but he delighted in the activities and customs of the city's local inhabitants. His scrutiny of the scene at Provost Street in winter renders this lithograph a telling visual account of typical town life in New York in the 1810s and 1820s.

Lithographié par Villeneuve figᵉ par V. Adam.   *Dessiné d'après nature par J. Milbert.*

Intérieur de New-York, rue de Provost et Chapel   Interior of New-York, Provost Street and Chapel

Urbs New-York intus adspecta. Provost et Chapel via   Das Innere von Neu York, Strase Provost and Chapel.

Imp. Lith. de Bove dirigée par Noël ainé & Cⁱᵉ

II.

View of Broadway, looking North from Ann Street, New York, as it appeared in 1819

1824

Carl Fredrik Akrell (Swedish, 1779–1868) after Baron Axel Leonhard Klinckowström (Swedish, 1775–1837)
Etching and aquatint, from *Atlas til Friherre Klinckowströms Bref om de Förenta Staterne*, published in Stockholm, 1824

Based on a captivating rendering by a Swedish aristocrat executed on his tour of the United States, this rare and masterful print (of which the New-York Historical Society holds a particularly fine impression) ranks among the most splendid views of the city in the first quarter of the nineteenth century.

By 1819, New York boasted a population of over 123,000, making it the largest city in America. This genteel stretch of Broadway, completed some seven years earlier, characterized the well-to-do city, with its handsome buildings (John Jacob Astor's house is the second on the left), nicely paved streets with distinctive pre-gas street lamps (left), elegantly landscaped squares, and a stately City Hall (right background). The latter, a remarkable synthesis of Federal and French Renaissance styles orchestrated by Joseph F. Mangin and John McComb, Jr., (1803–12), is still regarded as an architectural masterpiece today. The building is rendered accurately apart from the inclusion of the cross, which in fact never graced the building's cupola.

In addition to featuring New Yorkers going about their daily business, Klinckowström also included the roaming dogs and free-ranging pigs that shared the streets with the city's more refined inhabitants.

Ril. af Klinckowström.   Gr. af Akrell.

Brodway-gatan och Rådhuset i Newyork.

12.

Broadway from the Bowling Green

William James Bennett (American, born England, 1787–1844;
to New York c. 1826)
Aquatint, from *Megarey's Street Views in the City of New-York*, c. 1834

Bowling Green—a military parade area and cattle market in the seventeenth and early eighteenth centuries—became a small park in 1786, making it the oldest extant park in Manhattan today. In the early nineteenth century, the park was enjoyed by fashionable residents occupying the elegant townhouses lining lower Broadway. At 1 Broadway (left) is Kennedy House, where George Washington briefly resided during the American Revolution. In 1790, President Washington, with his wife Martha and a staff of servants, took up residence at 39 Broadway (the light-colored building shown further up the street). The spire of St. Paul's Chapel, the oldest church building in continuous use in New York, is visible on the right. The text that accompanies this view states,

> For local situation, extent, and
> beauty, this street is unrivaled on
> this side [of] the Atlantic, and may,
> perhaps, challenge competition
> with many of the finest in Europe.

William James Bennett was the preeminent watercolor and aquatint printmaker of his day, both in his native England and in the United States, where he settled by 1826. He drew this scene—his first of New York City—shortly after he arrived. Invited by the enterprising print publisher Henry J. Megarey to contribute to a series of twelve city views, as his first major American project Bennett retranslated this view of Broadway, along with images of South Street (plate 13) and Fulton Street, onto copper plates. These splendid scenes almost shimmer due to Bennett's exceptional control of light and dark tonalities.

BROADWAY FROM THE BOWLING GREEN.

Henry I. Megarey New York.

13.

South Street from Maiden Lane

William James Bennett
(American, born England, 1787–1844; to New York c. 1826)
Aquatint, from *Megarey's Street Views in the City of New-York*, c. 1834

The South Street waterfront, built on landfill and covered with cobblestones around 1800, was the hub of the city's successful maritime industry from 1815 until 1860. With extraordinary attention to detail as well as an expert command of overall composition, William Bennett depicted "a forest of masts" bathed in sunlight. Booms, bowsprits, and the interlaced lines and sails of tall ships crowd the port. Opposite, the sturdy row of brick mercantile buildings and shipping suppliers line South Street. Horse-drawn wagons and stevedores with small hand trucks transferred cargo to and from the import-export warehouses nearby. As the print's accompanying text declares,

> *The bales of merchandise, and the general appearance of bustle and life indicates the briskness of trade, and the growing prosperity of this great commercial metropolis.*

Wm I Bennett Pinxt et Sculpt

SOUTH ST. from MAIDEN LANE.

Henry I. Megarey New York.

14.

Merchants' Exchange, New York

1827

Alexander Jackson Davis (1803–1892)
Lithograph on chine collé, from *Views of the Public Buildings in the City of New-York*, printed and published by Anthony Imbert, 79 Murray Street, New York

Initially an illustrator for pocket-sized visitors' guides, in 1826 Alexander Jackson Davis worked briefly as a draftsman for Josiah R. Brady, a leading New York architect. By the following year, he had begun his own business as an "architectural composer," recording prominent new and historic buildings in New York City as well as providing drawings for other architects and builders. After 1830, the accomplished artist and printmaker moved on to design his own buildings in the Greek- and Gothic-revival styles.

Between 1825 and 1840, Davis documented many of the city's most important buildings in his lithographs.

Among his finest is this one, featuring the Merchants' Exchange. Martin Euclid Thompson (a carpenter-builder who had designed only one other major building), worked with Davis's former employer Brady to design the grand edifice in 1825. Their contemporaries deemed the building—with its colonnaded entry porch, cupola, and great interior trading room—"a superb structure." Its success not only elevated Thompson's professional stature but also distinguish Wall Street as the new commercial center of the city.

MERCHANTS EXCHANGE.
New York.

15.

The Ruins of Phelp's & Peck's Store,

Fulton Street, New York, as they appeared

on the morning after the Accident of

4th May 1832

Edward Williams Clay (1792–1857)
Lithograph, published by John B. Pendleton, 1832

Before photography, printmakers documented newsworthy events and sights, as well as disasters. In this rare eyewitness record by the lawyer-turned-political cartoonist Edward Williams Clay, bystanders and rescuers gathered at the corner of Cliff and Fulton streets, where the six-story Phelp's & Peck's Store had collapsed the previous afternoon, tragically burying several staff members. The weight of the store's inventory of wire and other metal products had proven to be too much for the floors to support, even though the building had been constructed only months before.

THE RUINS OF PHELP'S & PECK'S STORE,

Fulton St. New York, as they appeared on the morning after the Accident of 4ᵗʰ May 1832.

Lith of Pendleton, N.Y.

16.

View of the Great Fire in New York, December 16 & 17, 1835 as seen from the top of the Bank of America, corner of Wall and William Streets

William James Bennett (American, born England, 1787–1844;
to New York c. 1826) after Nicolino Calyo (American, born Italy, 1799–1884;
to New York 1835) Hand-colored aquatint and etching,
published by Lewis P. Clover, New York, 1836

How shall I record the events of last night, or how to attempt to describe the most awful calamity which has ever visited these United States? [It was the] greatest loss by fire that has ever been known, with the exception perhaps of the conflagration of Moscow, and that was an incidental concomitant of war.... Nearly one half of the first ward is in ashes.... The night was intensely cold, which was one cause of the unprecedented progress of the flames, for the water froze in the hydrants.

—Philip Hone, diary entry for
December 17, 1835

The Great Fire of 1835 started in a warehouse on Pearl Street on December 16th. By late the following day, approximately twenty blocks and more than six hundred wooden buildings—roughly one quarter of the city's commercial district located between Wall and Broad streets, Coenties Slip, and the East River— were completely destroyed. Although scores of volunteer firemen from Manhattan, Brooklyn, Long Island, and New Jersey responded, an inadequate water supply and unusually frigid temperatures prevented them from containing the fire.

Until the tragic events of September 11, 2001, the Great Fire of 1835 caused more property damage to New York's business district than any other event in the city's history. Remarkably, it claimed only two lives. This print serves as a picturesque visual record of this major disaster; the flames dramatically illuminate the path of the fire's destruction and the orderly brigades assembled to halt it.

Toward the left, the Merchants' Exchange stands in ruin, the majestic building that previously proclaimed the city's financial prowess reduced to a smoldering, gutted shell. Its loss, along with that of the stock exchange and the post office, seriously effected both the local and national economies: thousands were suddenly unemployed and hundreds were homeless; insurance companies could not cover all of the claims that were filed and banks struggled to make payments; prices for real estate, food, and other commodities rose sharply.

Yet within months of the great conflagration, developers secured sufficient funds to begin rebuilding. By 1837, New Yorkers had rebuilt many of the burned-out areas, and city leaders had reorganized the fire department. The immense Croton Water Works project was also launched to provide the city with a new, improved water supply, in large part to prevent a reoccurrence of similar tragedies of this magnitude.

VIEW OF THE GREAT FIRE IN NEW YORK, DEC. 16. & 17. 1835.

AS SEEN FROM THE TOP OF THE BANK OF AMERICA COR OF WALL & WM ST.

Published by L. P. CLOVER, New York.

Entered according to Act of Congress in the year 1836 by L.P. Clover in the Office of the Southern District of New York.

17. (RIGHT)

Ruins of the Merchants' Exchange after the Destructive Conflagration of December 16–17, 1835

John H. Bufford (1810–1870)
Hand-colored lithograph, printed by Nathaniel Currier; published by J. Disturnell, 156 Broadway, and J. H. Bufford, 19 Beekman Street, New York

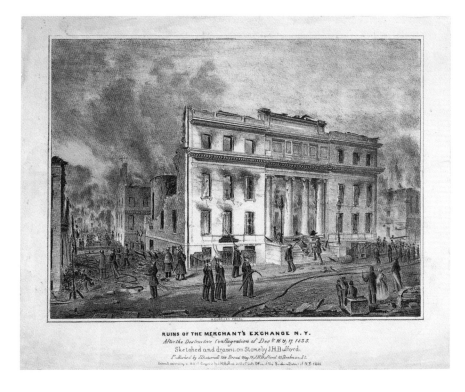

RUINS OF THE MERCHANT'S EXCHANGE N. Y.
After the Destructive Conflagration of Dec.r 16 & 17, 1835.
Sketched and drawn on Stone by J.H.Bufford.

18. (FAR RIGHT)

Merchants' Exchange, New York

1837

John H. Bufford (1810–1870) after an architectural rendering by Cyrus L. Warner (active in New York 1830–1850)
Lithograph in brown and blue-gray tints with selected hand-coloring

A year after fire consumed the first Merchants' Exchange, work began on the same site (now 55 Wall Street) to erect a new exchange building. Designed by architect Isaiah Rogers, one of America's leading architects from 1830 until his death in 1869, the monumental temple-like structure featured a raised colonnade of three-story Ionic granite columns on the exterior and a distinguished dome over the central trading hall inside.

Completed in 1842, the building became the U.S. Custom House in 1863 and was eventually regarded as Rogers's masterpiece.

The building still survives today, although it was somewhat transformed by the architectural firm of McKim, Mead & White, who renovated it in 1907.

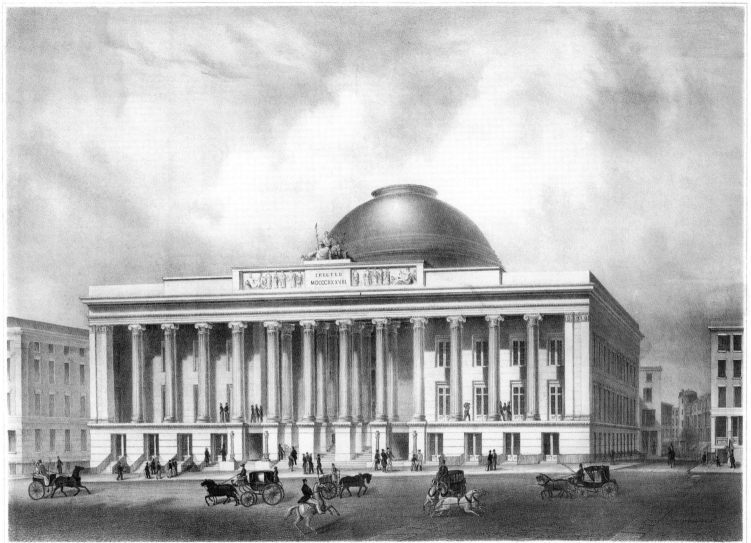

I. Rogers Arch.ᵗ   On Stone by Bufford.   Drawn by C.L.Warner.

MERCHANTS' EXCHANGE, NEW YORK.

New York Printed and Published at J.H.Bufford's Lithographic Establishment 136 Nassau St.

Entered according to Act of Congress, in the year 1840 by Ceo.L.Warner, in the Clerks Office of the District Court of the Southern District of New York

19.

Burning of the American Theatre, Bowery, between Four & Five o'Clock on Thursday Morning, September 22, 1836

September 1836

Unknown artist
Hand-colored lithograph, published by
H. R. Robinson, New York

When the Great Bowery Theater opened in 1826, it was the largest theater in North America and a potent rival to the renowned Park Theater on nearby Park Row. Although the Bowery Theater burned down several times (in 1828, in 1830, and, as documented here, in 1836), each time it was rebuilt and reincarnated, often under a different name. Its persistence helped to establish the Bowery as one of the city's main theater districts specializing in popular melodramas that appealed to immigrant and working-class audiences.

Entered according to act of Congress in the Year 1836, by H.R.Robinson, in the Clerks Office of the District Court of the United States of the Southern District of New-York.

BURNING OF THE AMERICAN THEATRE, BOWERY.

Between Four & Five o'Clock, on Thursday Morning, Sept.r 22.nd 1836.

Published September 1836, by the Proprietor, H.R.Robinson, 48.& 52. Courtland St. N.Y.

20.

New York from Brooklyn Heights

1837

William James Bennett (American, born England, 1787–1844;
to New York c. 1826)
after John William Hill (American, born England, 1812–1879; to U.S. 1819)
Hand-colored etching and aquatint, published by Lewis P. Clover, New York

This exceptional panorama of New York reveals the talents of two remarkable artists: here, William James Bennett applied his tour-de-force aquatint printmaking skills to translate the atmospheric quality and details of John William Hill's luminous watercolor. Shortly after Hill moved to New York in 1822 with his family, he received early art training from his father, John Hill, a skilled engraver; a little over a decade later, the younger Hill ranked among America's leading landscapists. From 1836 to 1841, he worked as a topographical artist for the New York Geological Survey, which accounts for the exactitude of this sweeping vista.

In the foreground, amid an architectural jigsaw of Brooklyn rooftops, a man and his family (he, with the aid of a telescope) take in the splendid view, encompassing the East River, crowded with boat traffic; the Manhattan skyline; the Hudson River; and New Jersey, in the distance. A stunning record of New York City one year after the Great Fire, this print features the new domed Merchants' Exchange (left), under construction at the time the print was made ; in his depiction, Hill anticipates the building's later appearance. A conflation of the present and the future, this print promotes New York as a great world city on a prosperous course of expansion.

Painted by J.W.Hill.

Published by L.P.CLOVER, New York.

Engraved by W.J.Bennett.

NEW YORK,

from Brooklyn Heights.

21. (TOP LEFT)

View above the Croton Dam, Plate IX

22. (BOTTOM LEFT)

Croton Aqueduct at Mill River, Plate XV

23. (BOTTOM RIGHT)

Croton Aqueduct at Yonkers, Plate XVIII

24. (TOP RIGHT)

View of the Jet at the Harlem River, Plate XX

William James Bennett (American, born England, 1787–1844;
to New York c. 1826) after Fayette B. Tower (1817–1857)
Four aquatints, from *Illustrations of the Croton Aqueduct,*
published by Wiley & Putnam, New York, 1843

These small picturesque scenes by master aquatint printmaker William James Bennett are based on drawings by F. B. Tower, one of the engineers for the Croton Aqueduct, a monumental project to bring clean and abundant water to New York City. Four of seven images Bennett made to illustrate Tower's publication on the history of the aqueduct, they document both the route the water traversed from natural source to city and the immense man-made structures especially designed as conduits. Among the very last prints Bennett made, these particular impressions are remarkably crisp and fresh: the water almost glistens.

New York was one of the first American cities to develop a reliable water distribution system for its citizens. Until the late eighteenth century, New Yorkers had been dependent on water of unpredictable quality and quantity. As the nineteenth century advanced, the private Manhattan Company began servicing a small percentage of the city's growing population via a convoluted network of wooden pipes. Firefighters relied mostly on water from city-owned tanks, the inadequacy of which gave rise to the Great Conflagration of December 16–17, 1835 (plates 16, 17). This disaster, along with frequent outbreaks of cholera and other epidemics caused by impure water, forced city leaders to pursue a project of unprecedented scale to obtain water from the Croton River, forty miles to the north.

The Croton Dam, aqueduct, and reservoir system was the most major undertaking of its kind in America. On October 14, 1842, New Yorkers celebrated its completion. Union Square and City Hall Park showcased spectacular jetting fountains, supplied by Croton water, as symbols of nature's bounty harnessed by human ingenuity and of the promise of pure and abundant drinking water for all.

VIEW ABOVE THE CROTON DAM.

VIEW OF THE JET AT HARLEM RIVER.

CROTON AQUEDUCT AT MILL RIVER.

CROTON AQUEDUCT AT YONKERS.

25.

The High Bridge at Harlem, New York

1849

Nathaniel Currier (1813–1888)
Lithograph, printed and published by Nathaniel Currier,
152 Nassau Street, corner of Spruce, New York

A triumph of architectural engineering for its day, the High Bridge (John B. Jervis, engineer, 1838–48) is here depicted shortly after its completion, surrounded by unpopulated countryside. Inspired by Roman aqueducts, this majestic arched stone structure spanned 1,450 feet and rose 114 feet above the high-water mark of the Harlem River. As this print's inscription indicates, the bridge, constructed at a cost of $1 million, was part of the Croton aqueduct system providing New York City with its first dependable public drinking-water supply. Until 1890, it was the only conduit for transporting water across the river.

Located just east of what is today West 174th Street, the High Bridge, which was partially dismantled in 1923, is no longer used as a water conduit. Thus, this vintage print provides viewers with an important historic picture of the oldest of New York City's great bridges.

Cost $ 1,000,000.
Length 1450 feet.

THE HIGH BRIDGE AT HARLEM, N.Y.

Height 114 ft from high water mark.
Began 1839, finished 1848.

This magnifient bridge of stone, forms a part of the immense works erected to bring the water of the Croton river to the City of New York.
The length of the aqueduct from the Croton river to the City Hall, is 44¼ miles, and cost about $ 13,000,000.—

26.

Croton Water Reservoir

1850

Charles Autenrieth (active 1850)
after Augustus Fay (c. 1824–?; active 1840s–1860)
Color lithograph with selected hand-coloring, from *Views of New York*,
printed and published by Henry Hoff

This colorful print depicts the massive fortress-like distributing reservoir that held water deposited by the Croton Aqueduct. The area where it stood was then on the northern fringes of the city, with only a few residences nearby; it had previously been a potter's field. Built between 1839 and 1842, the Croton Water Reservoir was situated on Fifth Avenue between 40th and 42nd streets (now the site of the New York Public Library). On July 4, 1842, at dawn, when water first flowed into the reservoir, the mayor invited special guests to witness the momentous event. The July 5th issue of the *Evening Post* reported that an immense crowd watched as the water was "successfully admitted at sunrise and continued to flow during the day, amid the roar of artillery and cheers of the multitude." The public walkway around the rim of the reservoir became a fashionable place to promenade and enjoy vistas of the city.

Publisher Henry Hoff issued this print, along with nineteen other views of New York, on sheets imprinted within an ornate gold border, thereby providing the public with affordable art for the parlor. Although the pictures looked like unique drawings, or miniature paintings, they were in fact made in large editions.

VIEWS
of
NEW-YORK

Drawn by C. Autenrieth.

Published by Henry Hoff. No. 120 William St. New-York.

Croton Water
Reservoir

Entered according to Act of Congress in the year 1850 by Henry Hoff in the Clerks Office of the District Court of the Southern District of N. York.

27.

Novelty Iron Works, Stillman, Allen & Co.
Steam Engine and General Machinery
Manufacturers, foot of 12th Street, East River,
New York

c. 1841–44

John Penniman (1817–1850)
Hand-colored lithograph, printed by George Endicott

Founded in the mid-1830s by Eliphalet Nott, who needed an engine built for his steamboat the *Novelty*, The Novelty Iron Works was by the 1840s the city's largest foundry specializing in steam engines for ocean-bound ships. This print promotes the foundry as a successful picture of industrial progress. By 1870, however, its machinery was outdated, and the factory closed.

In the early 1830s, the creator of this image—John Penniman—apprenticed with George Endicott in Baltimore, where Endicott had established his lithography printing business prior to moving to New York City. Sometime after 1840, Penniman came to New York and resumed working for Endicott. Described by a contemporary as a "clever and versatile designer," a "universal artist," and an "erratic individual," Penniman died in 1850, presumably due to alcohol-related causes.

NOVELTY IRON WORKS, FOOT OF 12th ST. E.R. NEW YORK.

STILLMAN, ALLEN & Co.
Iron Founders Steam Engine and General Machinery Manufacturers.

Steam Boilers Iron Ships and Boats, Sugar Mills, Wrought Iron Sugar Kettles
Improved Steam Clarifiers and Evaporators Vacuum Pans, Hydraulic

and Screw Cotton Presses Mill Work Fram new and approved
patterns, Brass Castings of every description &c &c.

28.

Panoramic View of New York, Taken from the North River

1844

Robert Havell, Jr. (English, 1793–1878; to U.S. 1839)
Hand-colored etching and aquatint, fifth state,
printed by W. Neale; colored by Henry A. Havell and Thomas P. Spearing;
published by Robert Havell, Sing Sing, New York,
by William A. Colman, New York, and by Ackerman & Co., London

Robert Havell came to America in 1839, having spent the previous fourteen years making the plates for Audubon's *Birds of America*. One of the most important natural history publications of its day, this epic work is also regarded as one of the greatest feats in the history of printmaking. Audubon's original watercolors and a rare set of the four-volume elephant folio of hand-colored prints (1827–38) are part of the society's collection.

In 1844, Havell created this sweeping view of New York as it appeared upon his arrival. It features the steeple of Trinity Church prior to its 1839 razing to make room for Richard Upjohn's masterpiece of ecclesiastical architecture (1839–46). The *British Queen*—the first trans-Atlantic steamboat, which had made its maiden voyage from England to New York in July 1839—is visible near the center. Crystalline in its overall detail, this print presents a captivating picture of Manhattan's waterfront from the west, across the North (or Hudson) River.

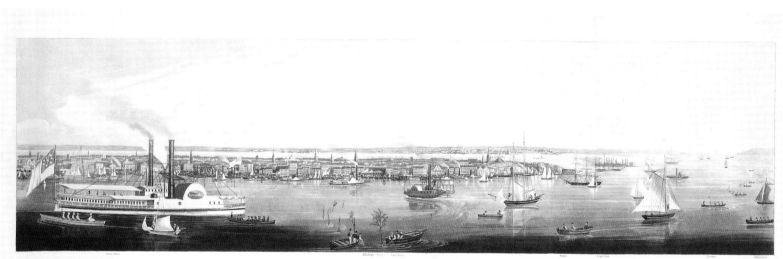

PANORAMIC VIEW OF NEW YORK.

29.

New-York Taken from the North West Angle of Fort Columbus, Governors Island

[as it appeared in 1844] 1846

Henry A. Papprill (English, 1817–1896; active in New York c. 1846–1850)
after Frederick Catherwood (English, 1799–1854)
Aquatint, published by Henry J. Megarey, New York

This prospect records the military presence on Governors Island, so-named by the British in 1698 when it was used "for the benefit and accommodation of His Majesty's governors." The imposing fortification, constructed between 1794 and 1798 to protect New York's harbor and rebuilt between 1806 and 1808, is shown with cannons at the ready along the fort wall and a drill in progress in the middle distance. The still-extant fort, now called by its original name, Fort Jay, was never actually used in battle.

NEW-YORK.

Taken from the North west angle of Fort Columbus, Governors Island.

30.

The New York Society Library—
Frederick Diaper Architect

c. 1840

G. Moore
Lithograph with tint stone,
printed by [William] Day & [Louis] Haghe, London

Established in 1754 for subscribing members, the New York Society Library is the oldest library in the city and the fourth oldest in the country. Originally located in City Hall, it suffered major book losses during the American Revolution. By 1839, however, its prospects had much improved, when it merged with the New York Athenaeum and moved to a new building at Broadway and Leonard Street. This print records the private library's elegant new Greek-revival building, the first major commission Frederick Diaper completed after arriving in New York from England. As his name is prominently mentioned in the print's inscription, he may have commissioned the work directly to proudly promote his architectural achievement.

Diaper went on to become one of America's most notable architects, designing banks, hotels, and houses until his death in 1906. The New York Society Library moved out of his building in 1856, to a new location on University Place; it still thrives today, on East 79th Street, where it has been since 1937.

G. Moore, del.

Day & Haghe, Lith.rs to The Queen.

THE NEW YORK SOCIETY LIBRARY.

FREDERICK DIAPER, ARCH.t

31.

North Interior View of the New York Post Office as it Appeared on Feb. 1, 1845

1845

George Endicott (1802–1848)
and William Endicott (1818–1850)
Lithograph, printed by G. & W. Endicott,
22 John Street, New York

This captivating scene of postal workers sorting the mail and distributing it into the rectangular banks of letter boxes is one of a very rare three-print series marking the February 1845 opening of the city's main post office on its new premises. Originally, the building (bounded by Liberty, Cedar, and Nassau streets) was the Middle Dutch Reformed Church (1721–31), which hosted the last worship service for its prosperous congregation on August 11, 1844. Because the neighborhood was filling with businesses, the church decided to lease the building to the federal government, which engaged Martin E. Thompson (the architect of the first Merchants' Exchange; plate 14) to convert it from an ecclesiastical space to a secular facility. The post office functioned in this building until 1875, when it relocated, and in 1883 the 152-year-old structure was demolished.

NORTH INTERIOR VIEW OF THE NEW YORK POST OFFICE,

LOCATED BY AUTHORITY OF THE HON. CHARLES A. WICKLIFFE POST MASTER GENERAL.

AND ARRANGED BY

John Lorimer Graham Esq. Postmaster.

FEB. 1st 1845.

ISAAC LUCAS, SUPERINTENDANT.   MARTIN E. THOMPSON, ARCHITECT.

32.

View of the Great Conflagration at New York, July 19th 1845, from the Corner of Broad and Stone Streets

1845

Nathaniel Currier (1813–1888)
Hand-colored lithograph,
printed and published by Nathaniel Currier,
2 Spruce Street, New York

In spite of the increased availability of water provided by the Croton Aqueduct after 1842, the city was still vulnerable to fires. In 1845 a colossal conflagration again struck downtown New York, destroying almost three hundred buildings. This print, showing a pair of fireman carrying a stretcher (center foreground), discretely alludes to the tragic fatalities: thirty in all. The extensive property damage, assessed at about $7 million according to the print's inscription, was devastating. New York insurance companies were unable to compensate the victims, hampering the city's economic recovery.

Nathaniel Currier, a lithographer from Massachusetts, opened his printing business in 1834 at the corner of Nassau and Spruce streets, where it remained for the next seventy years. After 1840, he stopped providing commercial printing for other clients; instead, he published and marketed prints created and produced by his own firm with its own artists. His shop became a meeting place for news reporters and those involved in various civic affairs, which gave him an advantage in offering topical pictorial prints "witnessing" New York City events. In 1857, he began his partnership with James Merritt Ives, and in the ensuing half-century, Currier & Ives became the most successful printmaking firm in America.

Lith. & Pub. by N. Currier,

Entered according to Act of Congress in the year 1845 by N. Currier, in the Clerk's office of the District Court of the Southern District of N.Y.

2 Spruce St. N.Y.

VIEW OF THE GREAT CONFLAGRATION AT NEW YORK JULY 19TH 1845.

Nearly 300 Buildings destroyed.

FROM COR. BROAD & STONE STS

Estimated loss of Property $ 7,000,000.

33.

Kipp and Brown's Stage as it Appeared in Passing the Astor House on the 16th Day of June 1845

1845

Henry R. Robinson,
lithographer (active in New York 1843–1851)
Hand-colored lithograph,
published by William H. Hoyt

On the afternoon of June 16, 1845, an omnibus driven by Henry W. Lacey and drawn by white horses, splendidly outfitted in silver-mounted harnesses, drove from 27th Street down Ninth Avenue to Hudson Street, via Canal Street to Broadway, where it continued down the Bowling Green and then returned back up Broadway to Union Park (now Union Square). This procession, reported in the newspapers of the day as a glorious spectacle as impressive as any gallant military parade, had the appearance of an official ceremony or civic festival; in reality, it was a grand publicity stunt concocted to promote Kipp and Brown's Stage Company as providing "the utmost possible in the way of omnibus driving." The following day, the *Evening Gazette* ventured a rebuke:

> *The twenty-two horse stage performed its tour yesterday, fortunately without accident to anyone. The skill with which this immense team of iron greys was handled, was certainly very great—but the inconvenience and even danger to the passers by was still greater, and therefore the feat ought not have been attempted. If our ambitious Jehus are desirous of showing their supremacy over all other whips, let them for the future select the country, or at all events some less crowded thoroughfare than Broadway for their display.*

This print features the glorious ensemble, which was 150 feet long from the nose of the lead horse to the driver's reins, in front of the city's first luxury hotel, Astor House (Isaiah Rogers, architect, 1836). This five-story hotel, located at 149 Broadway between Barclay and Vesey streets, boasted three hundred guest rooms and frequently hosted gatherings of preeminent statesmen and literary figures in its fine public rooms. With the prestigious hotel as its backdrop, this print served as a handsome promotional souvenir for both a fine mode of transportation and a fine place to stay.

KIPP & BROWN'S STAGE AS IT APPEAR'D IN PASSING THE ASTOR HOUSE ON THE 16ᵗʰ DAY OF JUNE 1845.

34.

The O'Connell Funeral Procession in the City of New York, September 22, 1847, with the magnificent cart drawn by twelve gray horses richly caparisoned with black cloth trimmed with silver and bearing a shield with the Irish harp

1847

James S. Baillie (active in New York 1838–1855)
Hand-colored lithograph, printed and published by James S. Baillie, 87 St. near Third Avenue, New York

During the 1840s, New York's immigrant population increased dramatically. The vast majority emigrated from Ireland, particularly in the decade following the 1845 potato crop failure. Of the 2.5 million Irish who came to America at this time, over one million came to New York City. By 1847, forty immigrant-laden ships entered New York's harbor daily. No city had ever before handled such a great flood of immigration.

Daniel O'Connell (1775–1847), the Irish national leader known as "the Liberator," had been elected a member of parliament in 1828 and later served briefly as Lord Mayor of Dublin (1841). He was revered by his countrymen both in Ireland and abroad, particularly by the poor, as he championed various reforms, including efforts (ultimately thwarted) to ease the suffering caused by the potato famine. In May 1847, while en route to Rome, he died suddenly in Genoa. In August 1847, when his body returned home, it received the honor of a lavish funeral.

This print documents the elaborate ceremonial funeral procession organized by the New York Irish as a memorial tribute to the great Irish patriot. Held on September 22, 1847, the procession began at Second Avenue, then meandered through the Bowery and down Broadway to the Battery, where a symbolic coffin covered with green velvet, richly embroidered with gold, was placed on a dais.

Printed in the September 23, 1847 edition of the *New York Herald*, the program included the music of marching bands and a lengthy eulogy by ex-Governor William H. Seward, who was said to have intoned,

It is a holy sight to see the obsequies of a soldier, not only of civil liberty, but of the liberty of conscience—of a soldier, not only of freedom, but also of the order of Christ—of a benefactor, not merely of a race or people, but of mankind.

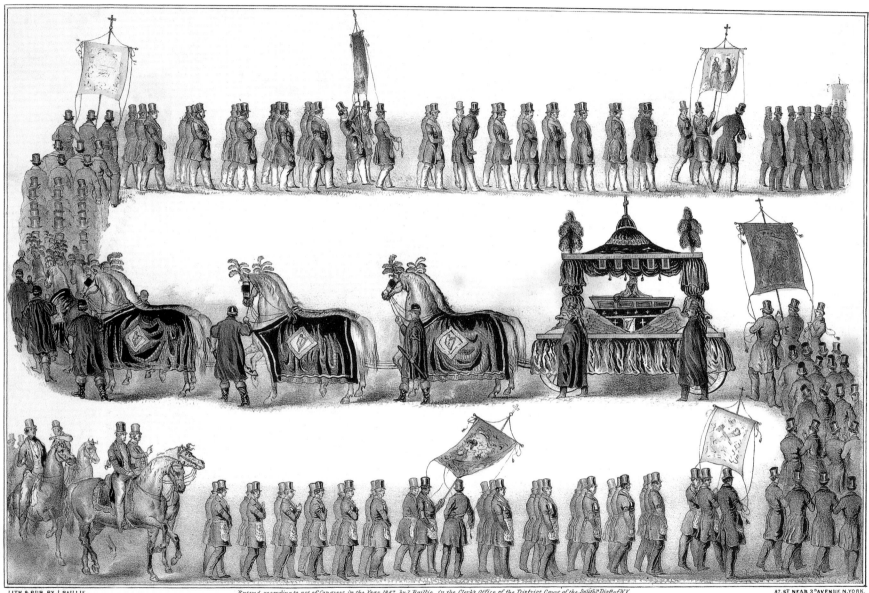

LITH. & PUB. BY J. BAILLIE,

Entered according to act of Congress, in the Year 1847, by J. Baillie, in the Clerk's Office of the District Court of the Southn. Distt. of N.Y.

87. ST NEAR 3 D AVENUE N. YORK.

THE O'CONNELL FUNERAL PROCESSION,
IN THE CITY OF NEW-YORK, SEPT. 22 ND 1847.

The Magnificent Car was drawn by 12 grey horses, richly Caparisoned with black Cloth, trimmed with Silver, and bearing a Shield with the Irish Harp upon it.

35.

New York City Hall, Park and Environs

c. 1849

John Bachmann
(American, born Germany, active in New York 1849–1885)
Lithograph, published by Williams & Stevens,
353 Broadway, New York

This wonderful view, probably from the roof of St. Paul's Chapel, presents the beautifully landscaped City Hall Park beyond a heavily trafficked, tree-lined Broadway. Some seven years earlier, on October 14, 1842, New Yorkers had celebrated the completion of the Croton Aqueduct, and for this memorable occasion, a spectacular temporary fountain that sent Croton water jetting skyward was installed in the park. Here, the permanent fountain that replaced it aesthetically proclaims the city's continued ability to provide refreshment for its citizens, while enhancing the setting of its most important municipal landmark.

The distinguished City Hall building (1803–12; New York City's third) was designed by John McComb, Jr., the first native-born architect, in collaboration with the French-native Joseph F. Mangin. Regarded as McComb's most important building, City Hall remains in active use today (plates 11, 83). A 1972 incarnation of the fountain marks the spot of the original water jets.

Bachmann del. & Lith.

Entered according to act of Congress by Williams & Stevens in the Clerks Office of the District of the Southern District of N.York.

NEW YORK CITY HALL, PARK AND ENVIRONS.

Published by Williams & Stevens. 353 Broadway N.Y.

36.

New York from the Steeple of St. Paul's Chapel Looking East, South and West

1849

Henry Papprill (English, 1817–1896; active in New York c. 1846–1850)
after John William Hill (English, 1812–1879; to U.S. 1819)
Color aquatint (in brown, gray, green, turquoise, steel blue),
proof, published by Henry J. Megarey, New York

From atop the steeple of St. Paul's Chapel (1764–66)—New York City's only pre-Revolutionary building still standing, located at the intersection of Broadway and Fulton Street—John William Hill made a magnificent watercolor view of Lower Manhattan which would serve as the basis for Papprill's splendid print. With Brooklyn, New York Harbor, and Staten Island in the distance, it shows how extensively built up New York had become by 1849. A year later, the city's population would reach seven hundred thousand; swelled by massive immigration, this figure was more than double what it had been in 1840.

The spire of Trinity Church commands the right (southern) part of this vista; at the center is the tower of the former Middle Dutch Church, which housed the city's main post office (plate 31). In the left foreground is P. T. Barnum's Museum of Sensational Curiosities; in the center foreground is portrait photographer Mathew Brady's Daguerrean Miniature Gallery (the skylights permitted additional light into his top-floor studio). Like a fringe, ship masts rim the island's eastern and western shores.

NEW YORK

37.

Great Riot at the Astor Place Opera House,
New York, Showing the dense Multitude of
spectators when the Military fired, Killing
and wounding about 70 persons

1849

Benjamin Franklin Butler
(died c. 1865; active in New York City c. 1846–1851)
Lithograph, published by Robert H. Elton,
90 Nassau Street, New York

The Astor Place Riot of May 10 and 11, 1849, one of the most serious riots in the city's history, began when supporters of the American actor Edwin Forrest disrupted a performance of his aristocratic English rival William C. Macready as he played the title role in *Macbeth*. The crowd's size and rage grew, fueled by thousands of disgruntled working-class men who came to rally against William B. Astor, then the city's largest landlord, who also owned the Opera House. Designed in 1847 by Isaiah Rogers, architect of the second Merchants' Exchange (plate 18), the building was extensively damaged in the melee. Police and New York State Militia were summoned when the violent mob failed to disperse; gunfire resulted in twenty-two deaths and many wounded. Martial law was imposed on the city for three days. One newspaper suggested renaming Astor Place "Dis-Astor Place."

Various printmakers quickly produced printed pictures of this catastrophic event in order to satisfy the public's curiosity. Although this image does not literally depict the agitation of the crowd, it conveys a sense of the setting, the immense throng, and the bursts of gunfire from the militia ringing the exterior of the building. This impression has a particularly fine inking in a rich, gunpowder black that complements the print's subject matter and renders it a vivid historical souvenir.

Pub.d at Eltons 90 Nassau St
Lith of B.F.Butler 96 Fulton St

GREAT RIOT AT THE ASTOR PLACE OPERA HOUSE NEW YORK

Showing the dense Multitude of spectators when the Military fired. Killing and wounding about — 70 Persons .

Killed							
Geo. W. Gedney	Aged 30	Mathew Cahan	Aged 23	Geo. W. Taylor	Aged 21	Geo W Brown	Aged 21
Wm Butler.	27	Owen Burns	30	Thos Kearnin	23	Henry Otten	
Neil Gray Mellis	27	Asa F Collins	45	Thimothy Macgaire	19	Andrew McKinley	25
Timothy Burns	18	Thos Burman	20	Kelly	—	Geo Lincoln	30
Geo. A Curtis	22	Thos Aylwood	19	Stephen Kehoe	24	Jno Meclennehan	—
Bridget Fagan							

38.

Awful Explosion of a Steam Boiler belonging to A. B. Taylor & Co. Machinists, No. 5 and 7 Hague Street, on Monday, February 4th at a quarter to 8 o'clock wounding and killing about 120 persons

1850

Charles Currier (1818–1887)
Hand-colored lithograph, printed by C. Currier,
33 Spruce Street, New York

Newspapers of the day reported that the Hague Street Disaster caused the greatest loss of life from any single accident or event of war that ever occurred in New York City: more than sixty people died, and scores of others were wounded in this steam boiler explosion in Queens. The tragedy prompted a committee of city aldermen to investigate the circumstances of the explosion. Like a news bulletin broadcast today, this rare broadside was issued immediately to notify a curious and concerned community about the event. Its powerful visual depiction of the horrific explosion was accompanied by a list of victims' names.

Entered according to Act of Congress, in the year 1850, A. D., by C. E. Lewis & Co., in the Clerk's Office in the District Court of the Southern District of the State of N. Y.

AWFUL EXPLOSION OF A STEAM BOILER,

Belonging to A. B. TAYLOR & Co., Machinists, Nos. 5 and 7 Hague-St.,

ON MONDAY, FEBRUARY 4th, AT A QUARTER TO 8 O'CLOCK.

WOUNDING AND KILLING ABOUT 120 PERSONS.

39.

El General Paez en Los Estados Unidos: Entrada del General Paez en Nueva York, Aug. 2, 1850

Francis D'Avignon after Albert Hoffmann
(French, 1813–after 1865; active in New York c. 1843–1859)
Lithograph with tint stone

This print's inscription hails and salutes General Jose Antonio Paez (1790–1878) as one of the first champions of liberty in South America, a distinguished soldier of patriotism, and a founder of the Venezuelan Republic. Shortly after General Paez's arrival in New York, Mayor Caleb S. Woodhull arranged for an official welcome and hero's parade, documented by this print.

The general's career reflects some of the vicissitudes inherent in Columbia and Venezuela's revolutionary history. From 1810 until 1820, as a guerrilla leader, he helped Simón Bolivar to defeat the Spanish in the South American War of Independence. The resulting new republic of Great Columbia included Venezuela; after Paez led separatist uprisings, Venezuela gained its independence, and Paez served as its first president from 1830 until 1835. He served twice again as president between 1838 and 1847, when he was overthrown and imprisoned until 1850. During the eight-year period of exile that followed his release, he resided in New York. He subsequently returned to Venezuela and became its dictator in 1861.

General Paez's warm reception in the city hints at the presence of fellow Latin Americans, and Spaniards, in New York City in the nineteenth century: between 1845 and 1870 their number increased from around five hundred to over two thousand.

The quality of this lithograph, by one of the most important print artists working in America at mid-century, is particularly fine. After arriving in the United States in 1842, D'Avignon, who had studied with one of France's leading artists of lithography, Horace Vernet, worked for New York's top lithography printers, including George Endicott and Sarony and Major. In 1849, he began a partnership with photographer Mathew Brady, in order to lithographically replicate photographic portraits. His work resulted in *The Gallery of Illustrious Americans*, published in the same year that D'Avignon created this print..

Litog. de D'Avignon, 323 Broadway.

por A. Hoffmann.

ENTRADA DEL GENERAL PAEZ EN NUEVA YORK.

Reconocemos y saludamos en vos á uno de los primeros campeones de la libertad del Sud Americano; al esforzado y valiente defensor de la independencia sur americana;
al distinguido soldado del ejercito patriota; al compañero de armas del gran Libertador Simon Bolivar, al fundador de la Republica de Venezuela; al digno presi-
dente de ella en dos periodos, al mejor apoyo, enfin, de la libertad civil.   (El Hon Sr. C. S. Woodhull, Mayor de la ciudad Agosto 2 de 1850.)

40.

First Appearance of Jenny Lind in America at Castle Garden, September 11, 1850

Nathaniel Currier (1813–1888)
Hand-colored lithograph,
printed and published by Nathaniel Currier,
152 Nassau Street, corner of Spruce, New York

Johanna Maria "Jenny" Lind's debut recital in America was the most spectacular performance ever held at Castle Garden. The celebrated *coloratura* soprano (1820–1887), came to America in 1850, after having retired from the opera a year earlier, to begin a career as a concert singer. She signed on for a two-year United States tour masterminded by show-man P. T. Barnum, who promoted her as "the Swedish Nightingale." At the center of this souvenir print documenting the tour's attendance-breaking inaugural concert is Lind, a tiny figure dressed in white sur-rounded by ringed rows accom-modating six thousand concert-goers. The print's inscription boasts of the concert's $26,238 total box-office receipts—an astonishing sum for its day—most of which Lind donated to charity.

The venue for the event was Castle Garden. Originally called Fort Clinton, it was erected between 1807 and 1811 to defend New York against British hostility. Designed by John McComb, Jr., one of America's leading architects of the early nineteenth century, it was converted into a grand theater for concerts and other public enter-tainments in 1823 (probably by McComb). The theater flourished between 1824 and 1855, after which time the building became an immigration depot.

FIRST APPEARANCE OF JENNY LIND IN AMERICA.
At Castle Garden Sept: 11th 1850.
Total Receipts $ 26.238.

41.

Bay of New York, Taken from the Battery

1851

Edward Valois (active 1840–1860) after John Bornet
(active in New York c. 1852–1856)
Hand-colored lithograph, printed by David McLellan,
26 Spruce Street, New York

On March 6, 1844, Philip Hone, a resident of Lower Manhattan, declared in his diary, "a more delightful scene can nowhere be found." He was referring to the view of the Bay of New York as seen from the Battery (now Battery Park), so named for the row of cannons once installed there to defend the southern tip of the island. This area first functioned as a public promenade in 1785, while New York City served as the national capital. This mid-nineteenth–century print shows the beautifully landscaped park full of fashionable strollers enjoying a glorious view of New York Harbor. At the far left is the Revenue Office and the Staten Island Ferry; at the far right is Castle Garden, a great entertainment venue located on an artificial island that was connected to the tip of Manhattan by a 300-foot causeway (plate 40). The vista in between shows Staten Island in the distance and the bay full of sailing vessels and steam ships, ferries and river boats, and even a couple of battleships.

BAY OF NEW YORK.

42.

View on the Harlem River, New York with the High Bridge in the Distance

1852

Frances [Fanny] Flora Bond Palmer
(English, 1812–1875; to U.S. 1840s), for Currier & Ives
Hand-colored lithograph,
printed and published by Currier & Ives

This idyllic view of the Harlem River features fishermen in the foreground, the 1813 Macombs (then spelled "McCombs") Bridge and the Toll House in the middle ground, and the great High Bridge in the background, up the river (plate 25). The viewer stands on the site near Robert Macomb's abandoned grist mill and dam, which had ceased operating around 1818. The bridge remained in use until 1858, when it was dismantled to make way for a new turntable drawbridge that would allow for greater navigability of the river. Today this area, on the Manhattan side of the 145th Street Bridge, is built up with residences and storefronts; a modern Macombs Dam Bridge is located nearby.

The creator of this print, Fanny Palmer, provided numerous images to Nathaniel Currier and, later, to Currier & Ives that became commercially successful prints. She was also distinguished for having supported her family with a steady income derived from her graphic arts career at a time when few well-bred women worked for a living.

FROM NATURE AND ON STONE BY F. F. PALMER.

LITH. BY CURRIER & IVES, N. Y.

VIEW ON THE HARLEM RIVER, N. Y.

THE HIGHBRIDGE IN THE DISTANCE.

New York. Publ.d by Currier & Ives 152 Nassau St.

43. (RIGHT)

The Old Brewery at the Five Points,
New York, as it Appeared on December 1, 1852,
Previous to its Being Torn Down by the Ladies
Home Missionary Society of the Methodist
Episcopal Church

After Charles Parsons
(American, born England, 1821–1910; to U.S. 1830)
Lithograph with tint stone,
printed and published by Endicott & Co., New York

44. (FAR RIGHT)

The Old Brewery at the Five Points,
New York, as it Appeared by Candlelight,
December 1852, When it Was Visited
by About 20,000 People

John W. Orr (1815–1887)
after Charles Parsons
(American, born England, 1821–1910; to U.S. 1830)
Wood engraving, printed by Oliver & Brother

The 1854 Ladies of the Mission publication documenting the construction of a new Mission House at the Five Points cited R. A. West, Esq.'s declaration that the demolition of the Old Brewery, which had once stood on its site, deserved "to be distinguished as a red letter day in the annals of our city's history":

> The great landmark of vice and degradation, the haunt of crime and the home of misery, will soon be among the things that were—a remembrance, but no longer a fact. In its stead will rise a landmark for virtue and morality, and a home for the disconsolate and the desolate. The drunkard, and the debased, and the stealthy murderer will no more hie thither for concealment, but sobriety, and purity, and mercy will stand with open arms to receive whomsoever will eschew vice and make fellowship a virtue. What no legal enactment could accomplish—what no machinery of municipal government could effect—Christian women have brought about, quietly but thoroughly and triumphantly.

Where today's New York courthouses and Chinatown now stand was once the neighborhood of Five Points, so named because of the convergence of five streets there, near lower Mulberry Street. The Brewery, built in 1792, had, by the 1830s, become notorious as a squalid slum; poor immigrants seeking affordable shelter continued to settle there throughout

THE OLD BREWERY AT THE FIVE POINTS N. Y.
As it appeared Dec' 1st 1852 previous to its being torn down by the Ladies Home Missionary Soc' of the M. E. Church

The Old Brewery at the Five Points, N.Y.

As it appeared by candle-light, Dec. 1852, when it was visited by about 20,000 people.

OLIVER & BROTHER, Printers, Marble Building, 22 Beekman-St, N. Y.

the 1840s. Dubbed a "den of thieves" and "murderer's alley," Five Points was ruled by gangs, and few New Yorkers dared to go there. By 1850 it was the most densely populated place in the country. The Old Brewery was its worst tenement.

The Ladies Home Missionary Society of the Methodist Episcopal Church formed the Five Points Mission in 1848, where it sponsored temperance meetings, a charity day school, and a missionary chapel for the community. In 1852, the society bought the Old Brewery building and scheduled its demolition in order to expand the mission. These prints document the Old Brewery in its final days. On November 30, 1852, the *New York Evening Post* announced:

> In the course of a few weeks the Old Brewery, on the Five Points, will be torn down, to give place to an elegant and commodious structure.... As the work of destruction will commence in a few days, those who have a desire to go see what was...the haunt of the most desperate thieves, murderers, and the abode of the most...wretched poverty, should not miss the present and only opportunity.

Prospective visitors were reassured that to better accommodate them, the building, which was still partially occupied, would be well-lit at night.

45.

Home for the Friendless, New York City, under the Management of the American Female Guardian Society

c. 1853–54

Francis Michelin and J. L. Shattuck
(Michelin & Shattuck, active as a partnership in New York, 1853–1854)
Hand-colored lithograph

The unrecorded deaths of family wage earners due to poor working conditions, accidents, disasters, and disease, coupled with a deluge of immigrant poor in the 1840s, left thousands of homeless and orphaned children roaming the city's streets. Because laws required arresting and institutionalizing these poor children, several private organizations developed to offer relief.

Founded in 1834 to provide temporary shelter for abandoned, needy children and destitute young women ("not fallen, but within the age and circumstances of temptation, needing protection, and willing to live by honest toil"), the American Female Guardian Society and Home of the Friendless opened new quarters on 30th Street between Madison and Fourth avenues in 1847. This print shows the classical style of the society offices and asylum on its site just north of Madison Square. The buildings behind included a chapel, a school, and a printing workshop to produce the society newsletter, which helped to bring in donations. The home would remain there (with additional buildings on 29th Street built in 1856) until 1902, when it moved to a more spacious facility in the Bronx.

HOME FOR THE FRIENDLESS,

NEW YORK CITY.

Under the Management of the American Female Guardian Society

46.

New-York Crystal Palace for the Exhibition of the Industry of All Nations

1853–54

François Courtin (French, 1820–1871)
Hand-colored lithograph, printed and published by Turgis,
Paris and New York

Inspired by the great success of London's 1851 Crystal Palace—which launched the phenomenon of the international exposition featuring multinational displays of industrial, technological, and artistic innovation—New York's civic and business leaders decided to sponsor an American Exhibition of the Industry of All Nations. The winning design for New York's Crystal Palace was a domed, cast-iron and glass building in the shape of a Greek cross by architects Georg Carstensen and Charles Gildemeister. As reported by the *New York Evening Post,* the first iron column of the exhibition pavilion was erected with appropriate ceremony on October 30, 1852, on a site facing Sixth Avenue between 40th and 42nd streets (now Bryant Park).

President Franklin Pierce opened the building on July 14, 1853, thereby inaugurating the first world's fair in America. Inside, more than four thousand exhibits from around the world showcased scientific discoveries, manufactured goods, and decorative arts, as well as steam-powered machinery, sewing machines, cameras, and other technological triumphs of the burgeoning industrial age. In addition to paintings, its public art gallery featured the largest collection of important sculpture ever to have been shown on these shores.

Tens of thousands of people visited the exhibition before it closed on November 1, 1854. As the groups in Middle Eastern and North African dress suggest, many traveled from abroad to see the fair. This charming print by a French artist was intended as a souvenir for French- as well as English-speaking markets, as evidenced by its bilingual inscription.

Paris V.ᵉ TURGIS,éditeur rue Serpente,10, et à New-York, Léonard S.ᵗ 99.   Lith. de Turgis r. Serpente,10. à Paris.   Lith. par F. Courtin.

 PALAIS DE CRISTAL DE NEW-YORK.

pour l'Exposition de l'industrie de toutes les Nations.

NEW-YORK CRYSTAL PALACE.

for the Exhibition of the Industry of all Nations.

47·

Latting Observatory near Sixth Avenue
between 42nd and 43rd Streets, New York,
Built as Part of the Exhibition of the
Industry of All Nations

1853

William Naugle (born 1817; active in New York until after 1880)
Lithograph with tint stone, printed by [Alexander] Robertson & [Henry]
Seibert Lithography, 121 Fulton Street, New York

New York City's first skyscraper and a forerunner to the Paris Eiffel Tower (1889), the Latting Observatory was conceived by Waring Latting and designed by architect William Naugle. At 350 feet high, the tower surpassed what had previously been the city's tallest landmark—the 290-foot-tall spire of Richard Upjohn's Trinity Church (1839–46). Constructed of timber braced with iron, the tower was erected between 1852 and 1853 on the north side of 42nd Street, opposite the Crystal Palace, as an exposition attraction. New York's first passenger steam elevator brought visitors to the tower's first- and second-story landings to experience a 360-degree view of the city and its environs. After the fair closed in late 1854, the observatory remained open (although it steadily lost money). It was destroyed by fire on August 30, 1856.

WARING LATTING, PROJECTOR.

W.ᴹ NAUGLE, ARCHITECT.

LATTING OBSERVATORY

NEAR 6ᵀᴴ AVENUE, & BETWEEN 42 ᴺᴰ & 43 ᴿᴰ STREETS, NEW YORK.

This observatory is 350 fᵗ Extreme height. Base 75 fᵗ in diameter form Octagon, & is capable of accommodating 2000 persons at a time on its various Landings.

48.

An Interior View of the Crystal Palace

1853

Charles Parsons
(American, born England, 1821–1910; to U.S. 1830)
Lithograph with tint stone,
printed by Endicott & Co.; published by George S. Appleton, New York

C. PARSONS, DEL AND LITH.

PRINTED BY ENDICOTT & C° N. Y.

AN INTERIOR VIEW OF THE CRYSTAL PALACE.

New York, Published by Geo. S. Appleton. 346 Broadway N. Y.

49.

The Destruction by Fire of the New York Crystal Palace, Oct. 5, 1858

Unknown artist
Hand-colored lithograph,
published by H. H. Lloyd & Co., and by Spearing & Stutzman,
Appleton's Building, New York

After the Exhibition of the Industry of All Nations closed on November 1, 1854, the Crystal Palace remained; manufacturers and other organizations continued to display their wares and art there. Although its builders and the fair's promoters had boasted that the building was completely fireproof, on October 5, 1858, it was entirely consumed by flames within minutes. The intense heat quickly melted the structure's iron framework, causing acres of glass panes to fall to the ground.

This rare print, which has survived its own ravages of time, presents a view from Latting Observatory as a dramatic record of the great inferno, complete with fleeing hordes, firemen, and curious onlookers. Over 3,900 exhibits were reduced to ash and rubble. As the *New York Herald* reported the next day, the cost of this monumental disaster was over $1.5 million in merchandise and exhibits—a staggering amount of money for its day.

THE DESTRUCTION BY FIRE OF THE

NEW YORK CRYSTAL PALACE,

October 5th 1858.

Published by H.H. LLOYD & CO. ALSO BY
SPEARING & STUTZMAN.   APPLETONS BUILDING N.Y.

50. (RIGHT [DETAIL] AND LEFT OVERLEAF)

Panorama of the Harbor of New York, Staten Island, and the Narrows

1854

John Bornet (active in New York c. 1852–1856)
Lithograph with tan and blue-gray tint stone,
printed by [Louis] Nagel & [Adam] Weingärtner, New York;
published by Goupil & Co., New York

51. (FAR RIGHT [DETAIL] AND RIGHT OVERLEAF)

Panorama of Manhattan Island, City of New York and Environs,

1854

John Bornet (active in New York c. 1852–1856)
Hand-colored lithograph with tint border, printed by
Adam Weingärtner of [Louis] Nagel & [Adam] Weingärtner, New York;
published by Goupil & Co., New York

This pair of spectacular aerial vistas shows the topography of New York City and its surroundings as it appeared in the early 1850s. Both panoramas are by John Bornet, a lithographer and artist who is cited in the city's directories between 1852 and 1856 but about whom nothing further is known (apart from his authorship of these remarkable prints and several others). These works demonstrate Bornet's extraordinary talents as a master of the bird's-eye view.

Bornet's harbor view (plate 50) features Manhattan (upper right) and Staten Island marking the city's Atlantic gateway. A line of ships entering and leaving via the Narrows indicates the city's connections to the rest of the world, which provided commerce vital to the city's economic and cultural well-being. The majority of immigrants also passed through the Narrows on the final leg of the journey that brought them to New York.

Staten Island, founded by the Dutch in the seventeenth century, is the most distant and geographically isolated of New York City's boroughs, accessible primarily by ferry until the 1964 opening of the Verrazano-Narrows Bridge (named for Giovanni da Verrazano, who in 1524 made the first recorded passage through the Narrows). In the lower foreground, a few of the large homes that served as country retreats for the well-to-do can be seen, as can the Quarantine Station, which over local protest had been situated there since 1799 to detain and treat seamen and passengers with infectious diseases. In the late 1850s, rioters protesting the quarantine's presence on the island succeeded in razing the building.

Bornet's sweeping panorama from the west (plate 51) shows New Jersey settlements and industries on

the west banks of the Hudson, in the foreground; a densely built Manhattan sprinkled with steeples and towers, in the middle distance; and the East River, Brooklyn, and the Narrows beyond. The inclusion of tracks and a train along the New Jersey shore underscores the recent completion of a rail system linking major East Coast cities and foreshadows the expansion that would occur westward from the country's largest metropolis.

At the bottom of the print, a legend identifies several landmarks in Manhattan, such as the Latting Observatory (toward the left), Madison Square and the Hippodrome (center), and Castle Garden (right off the tip of Manhattan). A pair of walkers on a country path in the lower central foreground suggest that rural pleasures still prevailed a short distance from the city.

PANORAMA of the HARBOR of NEW YORK,
STATEN ISLAND and the NARROWS.

Published by GOUPIL & C° 366 Broadway, New York.

CITY of NEW YORK and ENVIRONS.

52. (RIGHT [DETAIL] AND FOLDOUT)

New York

1855

Sigismond Himely (French, 1801–1872)
after John William Hill (American, born England, 1812–1879; to U.S. 1819)
Aquatint, printed by McQueen, London;
published by Francis and George Warren Smith, New York

From the 1830s to 1960, New York City ranked among the world's busiest ports. By the mid-1850s, the city's commercial well-being relied on an increasingly lucrative international maritime industry and trade, which, in turn, supported a multitude of domestic import and export businesses as well as local ship builders, suppliers, and repairers. This topographical print—a spectacular feat of large-scale aquatint printmaking—presents the heavily trafficked and easily navigable East River as viewed from Brooklyn. Beyond the picturesque yet factually depicted rowboats, sailing vessels, steam paddle-wheelers, and steam packets, scores of ships hug the wharves of Manhattan, which had become a densely built urban landscape. As revealed by this print, the city had grown tremendously since 1837, when the "Hill-Bennett-Clover View" (plate 20) was composed from almost the same vantage point.

This splendid impression— a rare one in black and white (other extant impressions are hand-colored)— forms the mid-nineteenth–century counterpart to the great eighteenth-century Burgis view of "Ye Flourishing City" (plates 3, 4). The 1852 watercolor by John William Hill upon which this print is based is also in the collection of the New-York Historical Society.

53.

View of Liberty Street, New York, from Broadway to Greenwich Street

c. 1855–56

Frederick Heppenheimer (German, 1826–1878;
active in New York after 1850)
Hand-colored lithograph

Frederick Heppenheimer made this print in order to promote Witte & Brunswig as fine importers of German and French fancy goods (including bracelets, beads, buttons, pipes, snuffboxes, walking canes, ornamental hardware, and "H. J. Neuss's celebrated needles and shawl pins," for which they were the sole agents). Also on offer was "a large assortment of accordeons [sic]." Probably issued to advertise the company's expansion to two locations (122 Liberty and 125 Cedar streets) in 1855, the print accurately depicts the store's facade on Liberty Street to aid prospective customers in recognizing Witte & Brunswig in its urban setting. The printmaker included several anecdotal details: a pigtailed Chinese man (lower right); a black man fashionably attired in plaid trousers, leaning against a lamp post (near lower right); and, cleverly, a man wearing placards advertising his own commercial lithography business (toward the lower left). Viewers today appreciate this print for its charming mid-nineteenth–century depiction of a typical New York City shopping area, filled with bourgeois pedestrians, horsemen, and carriages; it also provides a fine example of commercial poster printing via lithography.

Also evoked in this print is New York's German community, which comprised the second largest group of immigrants (after the Irish) making up the city's population. Between 1840 and 1860, more than one hundred thousand Germans arrived in New York. Witte & Brunswig's salutation "To Their Friends" is probably a direct appeal to their countrymen in the city. Commissioning this print from Heppenheimer, and thereby patronizing a fellow German, was a shrewd decision by a store that wished to support, and be supported by, the local German community.

WITTE & BRUNSWIG

122 LIBERTY &
125 CEDAR STREETS
NEW-YORK
TO THEIR FRIENDS.

VIEW OF LIBERTY STREET NEW-YORK.

From Broadway to Greenwich Street.

Lithog'r & printed by F. Heppenheimer, 22 North William St. N.Y.

54.

Scene in the New Russian Baths, No. 18 La Fayette Place

c. 1876–78

John Lawrence Giles (active in New York 1876–1882),
artist and lithographer
Lithograph, printed by Charles Hart

The 1842 completion of the Croton Aqueduct made bathing and personal hygiene easier for some city inhabitants, but the majority of residents who could not afford running water in their homes relied on public hydrants for their drinking and washing needs. Health and temperance reformers prompted the creation of drinking fountains and public baths to minimize the causes of contagious disease in the poorest sections of the city.

Like private spas today, some bath houses were established to offer special, healthful benefits and often catered to particular segments of the population. Dr. Edward Guttmann (1828–1896), a German immigrant who arrived in New York in 1854 to practice medicine, founded the Russian Baths on Lafayette Place in the mid-1850s. This print, made to publicize the establishment (after Guttmann had sold the business), shows off the facility's interior amenities to prospective gentleman customers.

Dr. Guttmann championed the restorative powers of the Russian vapor bath (a cousin of the Finnish sauna and the Turkish bath) as a means of rechanneling one's vital energy. Before reaching the United States, Russian steam bathing had been transplanted to Germany and France by Napoleon and his troops in 1812 as well as by occupying Russian troops, whose noticeable strength and vigor further promoted the practice of steam bathing. The first public steam bath opened in Berlin in 1818, and in subsequent decades a virtual bania mania took hold, as Russian baths sprang up in more than twenty major German cities and European capitals. In the United States, the Russian bath was most popular with well-off Russian-Jewish immigrants, as it both reminded them of their homeland and reinforced a sense of community in their new country.

SCENE IN THE NEW RUSSIAN BATHS N⁰ 18 LA FAYETTE PLACE.

55.

Sleighing in New York

1855

Thomas Benecke (active in New York 1855–1856)
Color lithograph with hand-coloring,
printed by Nagel & Lewis, 122 Fulton Street, New York;
published by Emil Seitz, 413 Broadway, New York

This boisterous scene of a sleigh
collision and snowball fight may
have been a staged spectacle, given
that it occurred in front of P. T.
Barnum's museum at the corner of
Broadway and Ann Street. Instead
of calamity, an ambience of winter
festivity is suggested by the spectators
and musicians positioned on the
museum's balcony.

56.

New York & Environs

1861

John Bachmann
(American, born Germany, active in New York 1849–1885),
artist, lithographer, and publisher
Lithograph with tan tint stone, printed by Conrad Fatzer

John Bachman was among a number of German lithographers who escaped the revolutionary disturbances occurring in Europe in 1848 by immigrating to America, where accomplished printmakers were in short supply. He quickly gained notice as a leading master of New York topographical prints, particularly aerial views. One of his most unusual is this drastically distorted circular image, based on a drawing he made from nature—possibly with the aid of a mirror or other optical device.

The central land masses of Manhattan and Governors Island are prominently featured in this startling global perspective from high in the sky, while the shores of New Jersey (left) and Long Island (right), as well as the regions to the north and south, melt away on the print's edges. In addition to a quirky smattering of ships in the bay, the viewer can make out Castle Garden, at the almost completely built-up tip of Manhattan, along with the long artery of Broadway, which skirts City Hall Park and its fountain.

Initially issued in 1859, the lithograph was reissued in 1861, probably due to popular demand. By this time New York was the largest and most densely built city in the United States: its population exceeded eight hundred thousand and together with Brooklyn numbered over one million inhabitants.

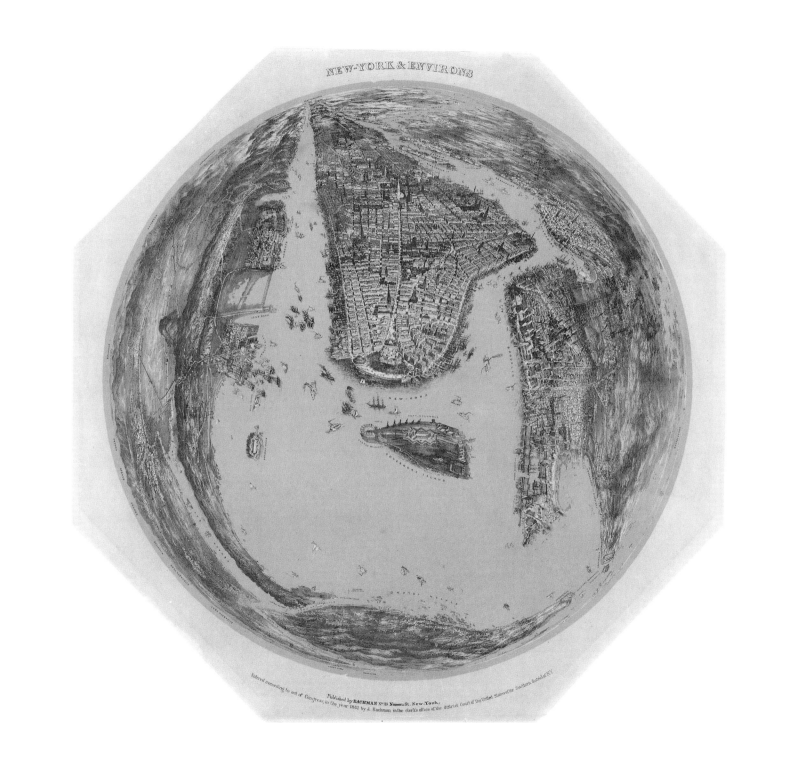

NEW-YORK & ENVIRONS

Published by BACHMAN Nº 115 Nassau St. New-York.

Entered according to act of Congress, in the year 1861 by J. Bachman in the clerk's office of the district Court of the United States of the Southern district of N.Y.

57.

Martel's New York Central Park, Respectfully Dedicated to the Park Commissioners

1864

Joseph C. Geissler (active in New York 1860–1865)
after Pierre (?) Martel
Lithograph with pink and gray-blue tint stones, printed by Henry C. Eno;
published by William H. Shields, New York

In 1858, landscape architect Frederick Law Olmsted and English architect Calvert Vaux provided the winning design for New York City's Central Park, the first major urban park and among the greatest public works projects ever undertaken in America. Years of massive earthworks, construction, and the planting of trees and shrubs, along with the insertion of architectural elements within the landscape in an unprecedented, artful way, transformed a previously neglected 843-acre expanse of open space, sparsely settled with small homesteads and shantytowns, into a pastoral woodland paradise. The public soon flocked to the park to experience this new "naturalistic" countryside filled with lakes, bridges, serpentine carriage routes, concealed underground passageways, meandering walkways, bridle paths, formal gardens, and picturesque vistas—a pleasing and healthful contrast to the city's densely populated urban fabric.

This incredible aerial view (possibly achieved via an observation balloon) depicts the southern half of the magnificent park: pedestrians and horse-drawn carriages scurry like ants through the park, and horse-drawn omnibuses line the street that flanks it. The lone building inside the park is the Arsenal (1847–51), by Martin E. Thompson, then a police station but soon to become the first home to the American Museum of Natural History. To the north (upper right), a reservoir holds the city's fresh water supply from the Croton Aqueduct. An admirable triumph of urban landscape design, the park remains a vital and vibrant oasis in the heart of the city today.

MARTEL'S NEW YORK CENTRAL PARK.

RESPECTFULLY DEDICATED TO THE PARK COMMISSIONERS.

58. (FAR RIGHT)

Sleighing in Central Park, New York City

After Thure de Thulstrup
(Swedish, 1848–1930; to U.S. via Canada c. 1875)
Wood engraving, from *Harper's Weekly*, February 18, 1888

59. (TOP)

Archway under Carriage Drive for Traffic Road across Central Park

c. 1860–64

Sarony, Major & Knapp, lithographers
[Napoleon Sarony (born Quebec 1821–1896; to New York c. 1836);
in partnership with Richard Major and Joseph F. Knapp, 1857–c. 1864]
Lithograph with tint stone

ARCHWAY UNDER CARRIAGE DRIVE
FOR TRAFFIC ROAD ACROSS THE PARK

This east-west street through Central Park was cleverly engineered as an underpass so that the park's carriage drive above would remain undisturbed by normal city traffic—here exemplified by a motley crowd and wayward sheep. All of the park structures, including the bridges, were designed by Calvert Vaux, a London-trained architect who moved to New York in 1856 and whose expertise ideally complemented the talents of his partner Frederick Law Olmsted.

The park's carriage drive provided an excellent site for winter recreation. An unnamed writer provided engaging commentary to accompany this sleigh-riding scene in Central Park in a 1888 issue of *Harper's Weekly*:

> One of the many surprising phenomena afforded by the city of New York is the putting forth of ten thousand sleighs, more or less, immediately after a snowfall. Some people might wonder that there should be any sleighs here at all, the quantity of snow we get seeming hardly great enough to warrant us in bothering with such things. But New-Yorkers have the cheerful disposition to seize upon a blessing when it comes, no matter if it is niggardly and infrequent. . . . For fifty-one weeks in the year, maybe, all plan of locomotion will need to be concerned with the problem of getting over the bare ground; then in the fifty-second week it will snow, and the sleighs will pop forth as naturally as though this were Montreal or St. Petersburg. . . . Mr. Thulstrup's picture affords us a vision of some of these handsome sleighs flying along the snow-clad reaches of Central Park.

SLEIGHING IN CENTRAL PARK, NEW YORK CITY.—Drawn by T. de Thulstrup.—[See Page 115.]

60.

Central-Park, Winter: The Skating Pond

1862

Lyman W. Atwater (1835–1891) after Charles Parsons
(American, born England, 1821–1910; to U.S. 1830)
Hand-colored lithograph, printed and published by
Currier & Ives

In December 1858, planners eager to attract people to Central Park opened the city's first organized ice-skating rink. The southeast corner of the then-unfinished park was flooded and played host to both men and women who, in accordance with convention, were required to skate in separate areas. By 1860, coed skating (as depicted here) had become an accepted—and fashionable—social pastime among the middle and upper classes.

CENTRAL - PARK, WINTER.
THE SKATING POND.

61.

Harlem Bridge Now Being Erected across the Harlem River at the Terminus of the Third Avenue, New York

1864

Endicott & Co., lithographer
Lithograph printed in gray, tan, and pale blue-green tints

This delicately tinted lithograph of engineer Erastus W. Smith's graceful, neo-classically inspired cast-iron bridge over the Harlem River marked the occasion of this remarkable structure's completion in 1863. Designed for carriage and other vehicular traffic, the 468-foot arched bridge—the first to be built on iron piers in North America—exhibited admirable engineering skill. The central span was designed to pivot on a ring of twelve columns, each six feet in diameter, to permit large boats to pass. At night, a central light illuminated the entire bridge when the draw was shut; when the draw was open, the light would turn to shine on the path of the passing boats.

In 1898 the bridge was replaced to keep pace with the city's modern transportation needs.

HARLEM BRIDGE.

NEW IRON VIADUCT ACROSS THE HARLEM RIVER AT THE TERMINUS OF THE THIRD AVENUE, NEW YORK.

CITY ENGINEER
ERASTUS W. SMITH

ARCHITECT
JOHN B. WICK

CONTRACTOR
CITY SURVEYOR
PUBLIC COMMISSIONERS
WILLIAM E. ROBINSON
GEORGE R. ROBINSON

62.

Presentation of Colors to the Twentieth U.S. Colored Infantry, Colonel N. B. Bartram, at the Union League Club House, New York, March 5, 1864

Unknown artist
Wood engraving, from *Frank Leslie's Illustrated Newspaper*,
March 26, 1864

On March 6, 1864, *The New York Times* reported on the event depicted in this print:

> *The scene of yesterday was one which marks an era of progress in the political and social history of New-York. A thousand men, with black skins, and clad and equipped with the uniforms and arms of the United States Government, marched from their camp through the most aristocratic and busy streets, received a grand ovation at the hands of the wealthiest and most respectable ladies and gentlemen of New-York,*

> *and then moved down Broadway to the steamer which bears them to their destination—all amid plaudits, the waving handkerchiefs, the showering bouquets, and other approving manifestations of a hundred thousand of the most loyal of our people.*

Less than a year earlier, an event of a different kind had consumed the attention of New Yorkers: the bloody Civil War draft riots. In July 1863, friction fueled by the complexities of abolitionist politics, the Emancipation Proclamation and the subsequent enforcement of federal conscription acts, intense anti-Negro sentiment among poor immigrants who feared job competition, and wartime hardships erupted in violent confrontations, lynchings, and brutal victimization of black people throughout the city. New York had lagged behind other states in recruiting and organizing regiments of what were then called Colored Volunteers. In the wake of the city's turbulent past, the organization of the Twentieth U.S. Colored Infantry—the first of its kind in New York—was a righteous triumph and vindication against lawless prejudice.

PRESENTATION OF COLORS TO THE 20th U. S. COLORED INFANTRY, COL. BARTRAM, AT THE UNION LEAGUE CLUB HOUSE, N. Y., MARCH 5.—PAGE 7

63.

Continental Works, Green Point, Brooklyn, T. F. Rowland, Proprietor

c. 1865

Endicott & Co., lithographer
Hand-colored lithograph

After 1840, Manhattan's unprecedented prosperity and growing population occasioned the displacement of numerous local industries and shipyards across the East River to Greenpoint, Williamsburg, and Brooklyn. Among the most important Greenpoint shipbuilders was Continental Works (also known as Continental Iron Works). It was established in 1860 by Thomas Fitch Rowland (1831–1907), a railroad engineer and fireman-turned-steamboat engineer who eventually developed expertise in producing marine engines as well as wrought- and cast-iron pipes.

Shortly after the outbreak of the Civil War in 1861, an engineer and inventor named John Ericsson was awarded a U.S. Navy commission to build the first iron-clad floating battery; Rowland's Continental Works was contracted to build its hull. The ship, christened the *Monitor,* was launched with considerable fanfare on January 30, 1862. Its victory in the first naval battle of the Civil War over the iron-clad Confederate *Merrimac* off the coast of Virginia assured Continental Works of further commissions.

The shipbuilding firm would produce four more iron-clad ships based on Ericsson's prototype, in addition to several more based on other designs. This print, which lists the Ericsson-inspired ships, may have been created to celebrate the launch of one of those later ships: throngs of people on the shore and in boats gather to witness the momentous maiden voyage of one of the most technologically up-to-date sailing vessels of its time.

In its heyday, Continental Works covered seven acres of waterfront and employed over fourteen hundred workers. After the war, military demand for ships declined, so Rowland shifted Continental Works's manufacturing capabilities to produce boilers, steam engines, and other equipment for the developing oil and gas industries.

CONTINENTAL WORKS, GREEN POINT, BROOKLYN.

T. F. ROWLAND, PROPRIETOR.

IRON SHIPS, IRON BRIDGES, BOILERS, TANKS AND GENERAL IRON WORK, VESSELS OF EVERY DESCRIPTION FURNISHED READY FOR SEA.

BUILDER OF U S IRON CLAD BATTERIES

1. Monitor
2. Passaic
3. Montauk
4. Sabine

5. Camanche
6. Dictator
7. Catskill
8. Miantonomah

64.

Submarine Mining Operations at Hallet's Point

1871

After a photograph by Rockwood & Co., New York
Wood engraving, from *Harper's Weekly*,
September 23, 1871

Hallet's Point (or Hell Gate, as it has come to be known)—the hazardous narrow strait between Astoria and Ward's Island that connects the East River to Long Island Sound—had been the site of scores of shipwrecks since the seventeenth century. In order to provide for safe passage through the strait (and thus improve the maritime prosperity of New York City) the government funded a major engineering project to widen and deepen the channel. This wood engraving (translated from a photograph to make the view cheap and easy to mass-produce) shows the dark caverns created by the dammed excavation—part of the preparations necessary for submarine blasting. A few years later, when the blasting finally occurred, it was purported to be the largest detonation in the world.

SUBMARINE MINING OPERATIONS AT HALLET'S POINT (HELL GATE).—Photographed by Rockwood & Co., 845 Broadway, New York.—[See Page 887.]

65.

The Port of New York: Bird's Eye View from the Battery, Looking South

1878

Charles R. Parsons (1844–1920) and Lyman W. Atwater (1835–1891)
Color lithograph, published by Currier & Ives

This extraordinary panorama shows New York Harbor swarming with a vast range of marine vessels—proof of the city's leadership as a world port. Castle Garden (by this time incorporated into the tip of Manhattan) and Battery Park feature prominently in the foreground. From 1855 to 1900, Castle Garden was used as an immigration depot, processing more than 7.5 million people. The daily influx of immigrants and the lovely scenic quality of the area explain the multitude of trams, carriages, and other vehicles carrying passengers to and from Battery Park.

THE PORT OF NEW YORK,
BIRDS EYE VIEW FROM THE BATTERY LOOKING SOUTH

66.

Coenties Slip, South Street

1881

F. Leo Hunter (1862–1943)
Etching

Once a thriving commercial district, South Street declined in maritime business after 1860, when its piers could no longer accommodate modern oceangoing vessels. Executed in 1881, this nostalgic view of Coenties Slip captures the wharf area, established by seventeenth-century Dutch colonists, free of contemporary urban intrusions and freshly dusted with snow. The atmosphere of a gray winter's day is beautifully evoked by Frederick Leo Hunter's expert manipulations of inked lines and surface veils of tone.

While lithography and wood engraving prevailed as the media of choice among printmakers for most of the nineteenth century, in 1877 a small group of artists founded the New York Etching Club to revive interest in this graphic technique. Hunter, who began as an architect and worked briefly in the firm of McKim, Mead & White, later pursued a career as an etcher, painter, and watercolorist, exhibiting frequently in the 1880s. Like other club members, he relished etching's capability to vividly depict street views, landscapes, and in particular, coastal scenes..

ADOLPH HUNTER.
MAR. 93

From the Original
drawing
G. Leo Hunter.
1881

67.

New York Tower (W. A. Roebling, Engineer) [under Construction for the East River Bridge]

September 1872

Unknown artist
Lithograph

German immigrants John Roebling (1806–1869) and his son Washington Augustus Roebling (1837–1926) pioneered the engineering of the suspension bridge—regarded as the greatest structural achievement of its day. In 1841, John invented a twisted wire-rope cable strong enough to support this unprecedented type of bridge span.

The most prestigious Roebling project was the design and construction of the first bridge over the East River, linking New York and Brooklyn. John Roebling was appointed chief engineer of the project in 1867, but he died two years later, the tragic result of an accident that occurred during the final survey for the bridge. His son succeeded him as chief engineer, overseeing the bridge's construction through its triumphant completion in 1883 (in spite of his own partial paralysis and other ailments caused by caisson disease, or the bends). The New York caisson was completed in May 1872; the tower above it, in July 1876. This rare image celebrates the technological innovation and labor involved in the massive construction of what would become one of the city's most heroic, and iconic, structures.

NEW YORK TOWER.
SEPT. 1872.
ENGINEER W.A.ROEBLING.

68.

Bird's Eye View of the Great New York and Brooklyn Bridge and Grand Display of Fireworks on Opening Night

1883

Unknown artist
Color lithograph in black, green, and red,
published by A. Major

On May 24, 1883, New York and Brooklyn officials hosted lavish festivities to celebrate the grand opening of the world's longest steel suspension bridge (just over 5,900 feet) that linked their two cities. Emily Roebling, the wife of chief engineer Washington A. Roebling and among those who helped to oversee the final phases of the bridge's realization, was the first to walk across the Great East River Bridge (afterward dubbed the Brooklyn Bridge). She was followed later that day by a troop of twenty-one elephants led by P. T. Barnum, in a combination publicity stunt and dramatic display of the weight-bearing capacity of the bridge. This print, depicting the great fanfare and spectacular fireworks that heralded the official opening of the bridge, was created as a fancy souvenir of this memorable event; its inscription contains key facts about the bridge.

A. MAJOR, Publisher, 822 Pearl St., N.Y.

JOHN A. ROEBLING, C. E.	DESIGNER OF BRIDGE.			WILLIAM VANDERBOSCH,	
WASHINGTON A. ROEBLING,	CHIEF ENGINEER.	NEW YORK TOWER.	BROOKLYN TOWER.	WILLIAM HILDENBRAND,	DRAUGHTSMEN.
CHARLES C. MARTIN,	1ST ASST. ENGINEER.			E. F. FARRINGTON,	
FRANCIS COLLINGWOOD,				THOS. G. DOUGLAS,	MASTER MECHANIC.
COL. WM. H. PAINE,	ENGINEERS.			CHAS. W. YOUNG,	SUPT. OF MASONRY.
GEO. W. McNULTY,					GENL. FOREMAN OF LABORERS.

BIRD'S-EYE VIEW OF THE GREAT NEW YORK AND BROOKLYN BRIDGE,
AND GRAND DISPLAY OF FIRE WORKS ON OPENING NIGHT,

[PYROTECHNICS FURNISHED BY DETWILLER & STREET, NEW YORK.]

COMMENCED JANUARY 3, 1870.   FINISHED MAY 24, 1883.

The Bridge crosses the river by a single span of 1595 ft., suspended by four cables 15¾ ins. in diameter; each cable consists of 5,434 parallel steel wires; ultimate strength of each cable 11,200 tons.   The approach on the New York side is 2,492½ ft., approach on the Brooklyn side 1,901 ft.,
total length 5,989 ft.   Size of towers at high water line 140x59 ft., total height of Towers 277 ft.   From high water to roadway 120 ft.,—from high water to centre of span 135 ft.,—from roadway to top 158 ft.,—width of Bridge 85 ft.,
with tracks for steam cars, roadway for carriages, and walks for foot passengers, and an elevated promenade commanding a view of extraordinary beauty and extent.   Cost, $15,000,000.

69. (RIGHT)

Under the Towers

Horace Baker (1833–1918)
after a watercolor by F. Hopkinson Smith (1838–1915)
Wood engraving,
from *Harper's Weekly,* February 18, 1882

70. (FAR RIGHT)

The Great East River Suspension Bridge Connecting the Cities of New York & Brooklyn, Showing Also the Splendid Panorama of the Bay and the Port of New York

1885

Currier & Ives (Nathanial Currier [1813–1895] and James Merritt Ives [1824–1895]; partnership formed 1857)
Color lithograph

These views of the Brooklyn Bridge, executed from the New York City side, provide a splendid record of the appearance of Lower Manhattan in the 1880s. The bridge's majestic towers, with their distinctive Gothic-style arches, serve as impressive gateways to each city, and its elaborate cable work gracefully supports the bridge's long span. In the Currier & Ives view (plate 70), a disproportionately large Statue of Liberty presides over New York Harbor.

Brooklyn Tower.

Fulton Ferry, Brooklyn.

Atlantic Ocean(in the distance)

New York Tower.

Coney Island.

Governors Island.

Highlands of Navesink(in the distance)

New York Cotton Exchange.

Produce Exchange.

Staten Island.

Mutual Life Ins Building.

Statue of Liberty
(on Bedloes Island.

Trinity Church.
Equitable Life Assurance Building.
New York Counting-house Bridge.

GRAND BIRDS EYE VIEW OF
THE GREAT EAST RIVER SUSPENSION BRIDGE.
CONNECTING THE CITIES OF NEW YORK & BROOKLYN
Showing also the splendid panorama of
THE BAY AND THE PORT OF NEW YORK.

Construction commenced January 1870 ..... Completed May, 1883 ..... Estimated cost $15,000,000

DIMENSIONS OF BRIDGE.

Height of towers	278 feet.
Height of Roadway (above H.W. mark) at towers	118 „
„ at centre of span	135 „
Four cables each 15¾ inches in diameter and each composed of 5434 parallel steel wires	
Strength of each cable	12,500 tons

DIMENSIONS OF BRIDGE.

River span, length	1595 feet.
Land spans, each	930 „
New York approach	1562 ½ „
Brooklyn approach	971 „
Total length	5989½ „
Width of Bridge	85 „

71. (LEFT OVERLEAF)

The Great Bartholdi Statue,
Liberty Enlightening the World—
The Gift of France to the American People
to Be Erected on Bedloe's Island,
New York Harbor

1883

Currier & Ives (Nathaniel Currier [1813–1895]
and James Merritt Ives [1824–1895]; partnership formed 1857)
Color lithograph

72. (RIGHT OVERLEAF)

The Great Bartholdi Statue,
Liberty Enlightening the World—
The Gift of France to the American People,
Erected on Bedloe's Island,
New York Harbor, and Unveiled
October, 28th, 1886

Currier & Ives (Nathaniel Currier [1813–1895]
and James Merritt Ives [1824–1895]; partnership formed 1857)
Color lithograph, copyrighted 1885; published 1886

Even before its realization, *Liberty Enlightening the World* (now called the Statue of Liberty National Monument) was renowned as a symbol of the freedoms enjoyed by American citizens. Following the proposal by a French statesman in 1865 for a joint Franco-American venture to celebrate independence and the alliance between the two countries, sculptor Fréderic Auguste Bartholdi (1834–1904) was chosen to execute the colossal statue. By 1871, he had selected Bedloe's Island (now Liberty Island) as the site of the statue and set forth its liberty theme. Between 1875 and 1886, the artist painstakingly developed the work from initial clay models to final castings in metal. He collaborated with the engineer Gustave Eiffel, who devised the internal structural frame needed to realize a statue of unprecedented scale.

Meanwhile, fundraising efforts took place on both sides of the Atlantic. By 1881, the French had raised $400,000 to realize the statue, but not until 1885 did the U.S. raise the $100,000 necessary to build the statue's base. Following *Liberty*'s display in Paris, the statue was dismantled, shipped in parts, and reassembled on Bedloe's Island. At the official New York unveiling on October 28, 1886, President Grover Cleveland formally accepted the statue as a gift from the French people against a backdrop of spectacular land and water parades. Anson Phelps

Stokes, who was among those on the platform with the President, related:

[Senator William M. Evarts] had got only part way along in his speech when the applause was mistaken by an eminent Frenchman present as the signal for him to pull the rope which unveiled the statue, upon which all the steamers and steam tugs which were in attendance about the island started their steam-whistles and the crowds on board them cheered, making a terrific din . . . Mr. Everts went right on with his speech, and President Cleveland, who presided, appeared as if giving strict attention to him, although it was impossible to hear what the orator was saying.

In order to capitalize on public interest in *Liberty*, Currier & Ives created several chromolithographs of the statue in advance of its completion. In the 1883 print shown here (plate 71), the colossal figure rests on an undistinguished hexagonal base, its final podium not yet designed. By comparison, the 1886 print commemorating *Liberty* at its unveiling (plate 72) shows its actual base—a stately granite pedestal with fluted pilasters designed by architect Richard Morris Hunt. Yet both prints picturesquely (if inaccurately) show Manhattan in the background, directly behind *Liberty*—an impossibility, given that the statue actually faces the Atlantic Ocean.

After the terrorist attacks of September 11, 2001, the statue of *Liberty* was closed for security reasons; this precautionary measure obliquely alluded to the fragile state of liberty rather than underscored actual threats against this majestic work of art. Today the preeminent New York landmark and tourist attraction is once again open to an adoring public.

THE GREAT BARTHOLDI STATUE.

LIBERTY ENLIGHTENING THE WORLD.

THE GIFT OF FRANCE TO THE AMERICAN PEOPLE.

ERECTED ON BEDLOE'S ISLAND   NEW YORK HARBOR

The statue is of copper bronzed, 145 ft in height, and is to be mounted on a stone pedestal 150 ft high, making the extreme height 295 ft   The torch will display a powerful electric
light, and the statue thus present by night as by day, an exceedingly grand and imposing appearance.

THE GREAT BARTHOLDI STATUE.
LIBERTY ENLIGHTENING THE WORLD.
THE GIFT OF FRANCE TO THE AMERICAN PEOPLE.
ERECTED ON BEDLOE'S ISLAND NEW YORK HARBOR, UNVEILED OCT. 28TH 1886

This magnificent colossal Statue (the largest ever known in the World) is of copper bronzed 151 feet in height and is mounted on a Stone Pedestal 154 feet high, making the extreme height from foundation of Pedestal to the torch 305 feet, the height of the Statue from the heel to the top of the head is 111 ft. 6 in. Length of the hand 16 feet. Head from chin to cranium 17 ft. 3 in. Breadth from ear to ear 10 feet, Length of nose 4 ft 6 in. Length of right arm 42 feet. Circumference of arm 12 feet, Width of mouth 3 feet, Weight of Statue 450,000 pounds (225 tons) 40 persons can stand comfortably in the head and the torch will hold 12 people. The torch at night displays a powerful electric light and the great Statue thus presents by night as by day an exceedingly grand and imposing appearance.

73.

Broadway, North from Cortlandt and Maiden Lane

c.1885–87

American Photo-Lithography Co.
Color photo-lithograph,
published by James J. Fogerty, New York

This bustling scene—created most likely to advertise a commercial district populated by merchants of jewelry, diamonds, and watches—is particularly interesting in its depiction of the criss-crossing telephone and telegraph lines and wires. The first telephone exchanges had begun to service Lower Manhattan in 1878 and were followed in 1882 by the first transmission of electricity. The proliferation of wires enveloped the city like a gigantic cobweb, prompting municipal leaders to advocate zoning laws that would require placing hazardous wires underground. Although city aldermen adopted an ordinance in 1883 giving electric companies two years to "bury" the wires, progress was slow, as evidenced by this 1885–87 print. Newspapers continued to cite complaints about unsightly and dangerous "overhead-wire abuse" in certain sections of the city into the 1890s.

This print also provides an interesting example of early photographically facilitated color printmaking technology (called photomechanical printmaking), which would, in the twentieth century, become widely used in the printing of magazines, advertisements, and informational, political, and cultural posters.

74. (FAR RIGHT)

Entrance to Brooklyn Bridge

1892

Charles F. W. Mielatz
(American, born Germany, 1864–1919; to U.S. 1867)
Etching on Japanese paper

75. (RIGHT)

Cherry Street

1904

Charles F. W. Mielatz
(American, born Germany, 1864–1919; to U.S. 1867)
Etching

76.

The Tombs

1889

Charles F. W. Mielatz
(American, born Germany, 1864–1919; to U.S. 1867)
Etching, later state

The cavernous entry portico of Manhattan's former House of Detention, supported by four monumental pillars in the form of stylized bundles of papyrus (or palms), was commonly called the Tombs in light of its imposing Egyptian-revival–style architecture. Designed by John Haviland and completed in 1838 on its Centre Street site (between Leonard and Franklin streets), the building was meant to handle two hundred prisoners awaiting trial, sentencing, or execution, but within a few decades its cells were woefully overcrowded and a larger, modernized facility was planned nearby. On the eve of its 1902 demolition, *The New York Times* reported,

[Many] have often wondered how it came to pass that the staid old City Fathers of those days went to ancient Egypt for an idea when they decided to build a new jail. But it appears that about that time John L. Stevens, a resident of Hoboken, had just . . . published . . . Stevens's Travels. . . . In it was the picture of an old Egyptian tomb which he had visited. The Common Council charged with the duty of selecting a plan for the prison and, wishing to make it forbidding in appearance so as to strike terror to those of evil intent, settled on the design in Stevens's book as one admirably adapted for their purpose. The result of the City Fathers' choice was described by Dickens in his

"American Notes" as "bastard Egyptian," but other writers pronounced it the finest specimen of Egyptian architecture outside of Egypt.

Charles F. W. Mielatz first issued this print of the Tombs with a waiting hansom cab in front of its stairs. Later—probably to emphasize this remarkable building and, perhaps, to make his print more saleable around the time of the building's demolition—the artist reworked the image, removing the horse-drawn carriage and creating the empty expanse of the plaza shown here.

77.

The Murray Hill Distributing Reservoir

1897

Edwin Davis French (1851–1906)
Engraving, published by the New York Society of Iconophiles,
January 1897

This view of the then-fifty-five-year-old Croton Reservoir was executed a few years before the structure was completely dismantled to make way for the New York Public Library (Carrère and Hastings, architects, 1911). By that time the metropolis had expanded into the Bronx, Brooklyn, and Queens, and the city had devised more modern systems for distributing water to its population, which numbered around 3.5 million.

Edwin Davis French began his career as an engraver on silver and later specialized in designing and engraving bookplates for private collectors and clubs. In 1895 the members of the Grolier Club, a private association of bibliophiles, founded the Society of Iconophiles, which sought to preserve New York history by commissioning artists to make prints of important city landmarks and views. French received the first commission, and this print is one of twelve he made for the Society of Iconophiles's inaugural publication. The society existed until 1930, eventually issuing 119 prints.

THE MURRAY HILL  DISTRIBUTING RESERVOIR.

78.

The Lych Gate
(Little Church around the Corner)

1902–06

Charles F. W. Mielatz
(American, born Germany, 1864–1919; to U.S. 1867)
Etching in brown ink on Japanese paper

That Mielatz's enchanting view of a church, a lone street sweeper in the foreground, depicts an actual site in New York, rather than in England or France, is almost hard to believe. Within its Gothic-Revival–style gate (Frederick C. Withers, architect, 1896), a quietude pervades the churchyard that today's viewers associate with a bygone era.

Characteristically, Mielatz placed the primary architectural subject of his print high on the picture plane, so that the undrawn areas of the image below (grazed with a whisper of tonal inking called plate tone) suggest the spatial expanse of the wet pavement and provide ambient atmosphere for the scene. Masterful etchings such as this prompted admirers to call Mielatz a "magician with the needle."

During the Civil War, the Episcopal Church of the Transfiguration (founded 1848 and more quaintly called the Little Church around the Corner), provided refuge to former slaves traveling on the Underground Railroad. Today this church, located on East 29th Street near Fifth Avenue, retains its air of nostalgic calm, tucked in between towering high-rises and slightly removed from the bustle of nearby traffic.

79. (RIGHT)

Restaurant in Mott Street

1906

Charles F. W. Mielatz
(American, born Germany, 1864–1919; to U.S. 1867)
Etching

80. (FAR RIGHT)

Balcony in Pell Street

1908

Charles F. W. Mielatz
(American, born Germany, 1864–1919; to U.S. 1867)
Four-color etching, second state, on Japanese paper

Throughout his career, Charles F. W. Mielatz explored the increasingly multinational city of New York in search of picturesque views. His refined prints convey his sense of wonder as he discovered new and culturally diverse neighborhoods. These two views, featuring Chinatown's ornate balconies as a backdrop for pedestrians clothed in their native dress, capture the exoticism of the Orient, which appealed to the artist and to Western print collectors alike.

The first Chinese to come to New York were sailors and merchants—purveyors of the eighteenth-century China trade who rarely stayed on. Beginning in 1848, a small number of Chinese men were allowed to immigrate, settling within the small area of Pell, Doyers, and Mott streets in Lower Manhattan. They were prevented by immigration laws from marrying or becoming citizens initially, and they were only allowed to open a few types of businesses, such as hand laundries and grocery stores. By the end of the nineteenth century, the population had grown, and restaurants and shops selling Chinese curios, silk, and porcelain had developed for tourists. When Mielatz made these prints in the 1900s, several thousand Chinese immigrants inhabited New York's Chinatown.

81. (RIGHT)

Rebuilding Fifth Avenue

1908

Joseph Pennell (1857–1926)
Etching

82. (FAR RIGHT)

St. Paul's, New York

1915

Joseph Pennell (1857–1926)
Etching

Philadelphia-born artist Joseph Pennell, one of the chief figures of the American etching revival, commenced printmaking in 1877, inspired by the wonderful impressions he saw by James McNeill Whistler and other master etchers working in Europe. In 1883, when he first traveled to the Continent, he made a group of etchings of picturesque sights that launched his successful graphic career. His 1884 meeting with Whistler further fueled Pennell's passion to emulate the artist's etching process and print connoisseurship, which included skilled drawing directly onto the etching plate, carefully nuanced inking, and printing onto quality paper. An ardent disciple, Pennell promoted Whistler in America and later wrote a biography of the master. In addition to being a prolific printmaker, Pennell also became an influential proponent of the fine art of printmaking.

In Pennell's richly inked etching of St. Paul's Chapel (plate 82), the 1794 steeple that once commanded the skyline at Broadway at Fulton Street is dwarfed by modern structures under construction. The erection of the commercial Fifth Avenue Building at Twenty-third Street, where the once-popular Fifth Avenue Hotel had stood until 1907 is the subject of another notable print (plate 81). This building remains in use today.

Pennell created over fifteen hundred etchings and lithographs, primarily featuring buildings and city views like these. He recorded the dramatic changes taking place within the topography of New York in the 1900s and 1910s, as new construction expanded the city's commercial area not only northward but skyward.

83.

City Hall Park

1911

Henri Deville (French, 1871–?;
active in U.S. 1902–1914)
Etching

H Deville

-II-

3/25   H Deville imp

84. (RIGHT)

Washington Arch

1 9 2 3

John Sloan (1871–1951)
Etching

85. (FAR RIGHT)

Easter Eve, Washington Square

1 9 2 6

John Sloan (1871–1951)
Etching and aquatint (on zinc)

John Sloan was among the first American painters and etchers to use his observations of ordinary New York City life as the chief subject of his art. After teaching himself the rudiments of etching from a standard how-to manual, he made ten prints for a series titled *New York City Life* (1905–06). Encouraged by the popular success of those prints, he continued to look to the city for inspiration. In 1908,

together with other artists known as the Ashcan School, he shocked the traditional art world with a display of gritty, realistic paintings of unremarkable urban scenes. In a matter of decades, Sloan's realist paintings and prints came to be regarded as masterpieces of early twentieth-century American art.

These captivating prints by Sloan feature the everyday life of New Yorkers in Washington Square Park. McKim, Mead & White's Memorial Arch (1892; originally erected in wood for the 1889 centennial celebration of George Washington's inauguration) provided an elegant backdrop to the scenes.

Sloan lived and worked near the arch, but he also had a deeper connection with the landmark, an outgrowth of his socialist political leanings. On the evening of January 23, 1917, Sloan and a small group of his bohemian friends (including Marcel Duchamp) decorated the marble arch with candles and climbed to its summit, where, while enjoying a midnight picnic, they proclaimed that Greenwich Village was seceding from the United States and would thence forth be known as the Free and Independent Republic of Washington Square. The door to the arch's stairway was kept locked thereafter to prevent further unauthorized ascents.

Washington Arch.

100 proofs

John Sloan, 1926.

Easter Eve.

86.

Williamsburg Bridge

July 4, 1924

Frederick K. Detwiller (1882–1953)
Etching and aquatint

The second bridge built to span the East River, the Williamsburg Bridge opened in December 1903. Designed primarily by the engineer Leffert L. Buck, it was the first steel suspension bridge; its latticework towers and span (which incorporated a pair of subway tracks flanked by traffic lanes) made it the heaviest bridge in the world. Although many critics deemed its design ungainly, the bridge eased access between the Lower East Side and Williamsburg, thereby facilitating the migration of residents from an overcrowded Manhattan to Brooklyn. Frederick K. Detwiller's Independence Day print presents a somewhat quirky view of vehicles (including a lone horse-drawn wagon) traversing the river.

Initially trained as a lawyer, in 1907 Detwiller pursued a career in art and architecture, first at Columbia University and then at the Paris École des Beaux-Arts. His obituary described the professional painter and print-maker as a lively observer of the New York scene as well as an active advocate for local causes; for example, he was known to have railed against Greenwich Village landlords for raising rents and thereby preventing struggling artists from living there.

Help Complete New York's Great Cathedral, A Shrine of Worship for all People

1925

Adolf Treidler (1886–1981)
Color lithograph poster, published by Carey & Sons

Building the Nave, Cathedral of St. John the Divine, New York City

June 1925

Frederick K. Detwiller (1882–1953)
Etching and aquatint

By 1925, when this print and poster were issued, more than three decades had elapsed since building commenced on the Cathedral of St. John the Divine. These images document the community's renewed efforts after a long hiatus to complete the nation's largest church.

The idea for the grandiose edifice dated to 1887, when the newly appointed Bishop Henry Codman Potter appealed to New Yorkers to support the building of a new Episcopal cathedral in Morningside Heights, on a site with a commanding view of the city. What began with great promise soon devolved into a drawn-out process of compromised designs, intermittent construction, cost overruns, and funding delays, leaving a building with sections unfinished. The young architectural firm of Heins & La Farge was handed the commission in 1891 and construction began again in 1893, but disagreements over key design decisions strained church relations with the architects and slowed progress. By 1911, a Byzantine-Romanesque–style apse, choir, and crossing were completed, as depicted in Frederick K. Detwiller's print. The crossing's impressive vaulting (designed by Raphael Guastavino) provided a temporary roof until the tower could be erected.

Subsequent architectural disputes led to the re-assigning of the project to Ralph Adams Cram, a Gothic-revival advocate with the firm of Cram & Wentworth in Boston. He redesigned the nave and west facade of the cathedral, but construction could not be resumed due to a lack of funds. In 1925, Franklin D. Roosevelt launched a massive $15 million fundraising campaign to finance the work on the "shrine of worship for all people." The poster by Adolf Treidler documented this historic appeal and presented a stunning vision of the majestic, five-portal Gothic facade silhouetted against the starry heavens. The successful campaign funded construction throughout the Depression, resulting in the completion of the nave and west facade in 1941.

© Building the New Cathedral of St. John the Divine New York City June 1925

89.

Building with Steel, Paramount Building
on Broadway between 43rd to 44th Streets

1926

William C. McNulty (1889–1963)
Drypoint

By exploiting the strength of steel in its structural framework, the tall office building grew into the skyscraper, with the addition of more floors translating into more available real estate. The thirty-three–story Paramount Building (Rapp & Rapp, architect), shown under construction here, would become the tallest building on Broadway north of the Woolworth Building (plates 98, 99) when completed in 1927.

By including passing streetcars and pedestrians in his view, the artist conveyed the grand scale of the building's lower levels. Once housing the Paramount Theater, the structure held offices for the Famous Players-Lasky Corporation (later Paramount Pictures), which represented film stars such as Clara Bow, Gloria Swanson, and Rudolph Valentino. The building still stands in Times Square today.

Building with Steel. Paramount Bldg. B'way 43d to 44th S. 1926

Wm C. McNulty imp

No 105

90.

Demolishing Old Madison Square Garden,
Fourth Avenue and 26th Street

1927

William C. McNulty (1889–1963)
Drypoint and etching, trial proof

The glorious terra-cotta–ornamented, Moorish-Spanish–style Madison Square Garden was designed by Stanford White and built by the firm of McKim, Mead & White between 1887 and 1891. Located on the former site of P. T. Barnum's Hippodrome, the building boasted the country's largest auditorium, where it hosted horse shows, dog shows, bicycle races, circuses, boxing matches, and political conventions. It also possessed a theater, concert hall, large restaurant, and roof-garden cabaret (which was the site of White's sensational murder at the hands of his mistress' jealous husband in 1906). Its tower, modeled on the Giralda in Seville, is among the only features still standing in this 1927 print, which documents the demolition of this architectural masterpiece two years earlier to make way for the new headquarters of the New York Life Insurance Company (Cass Gilbert, architect, 1928). A new Madison Square Garden was built on Eighth Avenue (between 49th and 50th streets) before eventually moving to its current location at Pennsylvania Station.

Demolishing Old Madison Square Garden
Trial Proof. 1927

Wm. C. McNulty imp.

91.

Demolishing the Century Theatre,
Central Park West and 63rd Street

1930

William C. McNulty (1889–1963)
Drypoint

In December 1908, the cornerstone of Carrère and Hastings's New Theatre (later renamed the Century Theatre) was laid with considerable ceremony and to-do. Following a reading of special greetings from President Theodore Roosevelt, New York Governor Charles Evans Hughes proclaimed,

> *This enterprise, which promises so much for the promotion of dramatic art and contemplates the addition to our city of a new theatre building notable for its architectural beauty and adaptation, cannot fail to be of great value in the development of our city life.*

In spite of these auspicious beginnings, the noble edifice proved unprofitable; it was demolished to make way for a new Art Deco apartment building, designed by the office of Irwin S. Chanin; christened Century Apartments, its name honors the previous inhabitant of the site.

William McNulty's wonderful impression evokes the deep shadows of the night, contrasted with illumination that plays across the theater's picturesque ruins. Recalling ancient Rome, the image eloquently documents the demise of one of New York's great theater buildings.

Demolishing The Century Theatre 1931   Wm McNulty
70 Proofs
Central Park West & 62 St

92.

Metropolis from Governors Island

c. 1927

Anton Schutz
(American, born Germany, 1894–1977; to U.S. 1924)
Etching

An accomplished etcher of architectural views of New York and other major cities, Anton Schutz learned his craft while studying architecture in Munich. In 1924, he emigrated to the United States and on his second day in New York met Joseph Pennell. Shortly afterward, he became Pennell's printing assistant. Throughout the 1920s and early 1930s, the literal precision of his own etchings were favorably received, earning his work a regular place in gallery and etching society exhibitions in New York, Brooklyn, Chicago, and Philadelphia.

Schutz supplemented the income from his etching career by founding his own business in 1925: the New York Graphic Society. Initially intent on marketing original graphic art, by the mid-1940s the society had become the world's largest publisher of color art reproductions. (Time, Inc. would purchase Schutz's brainchild in 1966.)

The architectural prints created by Schutz and his peers served as both visual rhapsodies on and graphic witnesses to the burgeoning modern metropolis.

93. (RIGHT)

Gateway to Wall Street at Broadway

1930

Anton Schutz
(American, born Germany, 1894–1977; to U.S. 1924)
Etching

Wall Street, formerly the northern boundary of colonial New Amsterdam, became in the modern era the locus of the financial industry, synonymous with the profession. The Irving Trust Company building (Voorhees, Gmelin & Walker, architect, completed 1932) at the corner of Wall Street and Broadway greeted visitors in Schutz's day (as today), its curving wall of "Gothic" portals acting as a gateway to the world of high finance beyond.

94. (FAR RIGHT)

New York Stock Exchange

1927

Tavik František Šimon
(Bohemian, 1877–1942)
Color soft-ground etching and aquatint

Since the 1790s, New York City has dominated the national and international securities market. A successor to the Merchants' Exchange, this impressive neo-classical building designed by George B. Post for a site at Broad and Wall streets has housed the New York Stock Exchange since its completion in 1903. Its temple facade projects a sense of enduring strength, power, and dignity—qualities required to ride out the daily vicissitudes of high finance. To underscore this point, sculptural figures personifying *Agriculture, Mining, Science, Industry,* and *Invention* flank *Integrity Protecting the Works of Man* above the building's massive colonnade.

As a European visiting New York in 1927, Tavik František Šimon was impressed by the city's dynamism and aura of modern progress, epitomized by Wall Street. In his print, the artist hinted at future changes to the cityscape with the inclusion of a crane (right).

95. (BOTTOM)

Interior of the Stock Exchange

Joseph W. Golinken (1896–1977)
Lithograph

96. (RIGHT)

Floor of the Stock Exchange

January 7, 8, and 9, 1927

Childe Hassam (1859–1935)
Etching

The floor of the New York Stock Exchange is renowned for the frenzied, almost raucous activity that goes on there, which drives the country's major investment trading. A skilled draftsman, Joseph Golinken evoked the vigorous commotion that typifies life on the trading floor in his lithograph (left).

Childe Hassam, the celebrated American Impressionist, also depicted the interior of the exchange, in an earlier etching. His view—one of the few he did that features the economic life of the city—captures a less typical scene. Set just prior to the opening bell, just after the closing bell, or perhaps during an uncharacteristic lull in the action, Hassam's print resonates with an aura of calm.

A comparison of these prints also reveals nuances of the printmaking techniques employed by each artist: etching permitted Hassam to draw his sedate scene with a precise linearity, while lithography offered Golinkin a means to more fluidly draw and shade his circus of gesturing figures.

To Kilian Van Rensselaer from Childe Hassam

97.

New York-Brooklyn Bridge

1927

Tavik František Šimon
(Bohemian, 1877–1942)
Color soft-ground etching and aquatint

After studying painting in Prague, Tavik František Šimon pursued an art career, primarily in Paris, after 1903. He was so inspired by contemporary French color printmaking that he began to develop his own style of color aquatint. Using this technique, he eventually executed over six hundred prints featuring the picturesque city views he encountered in Paris as well as on his extensive travels throughout Europe, Morocco, Ceylon, India, Japan, and the United States. He made about seven prints after his 1927 visit to New York City, this lyrical view among them. While his prints were quite popular in his own day,

earning him a reputation as a leading twentieth-century printmaker in his homeland, he is less well known today in this country.

This exquisitely printed twilight view of the Lower Manhattan skyline, depicting the Woolworth Building as a soaring spire, is one of Šimon's best. It captures the rhapsodizing beauty of the Brooklyn Bridge (foreground) and the spectacular urban panorama beyond that has inspired the work of countless artists, musicians, writers, and poets for the past century.

T. F. Šimon

98. (RIGHT)

Woolworth Building, New York

1929

William C. McNulty (1889–1963)
Drypoint

Created by Cass Gilbert between 1911 and 1913 and dubbed the "Mozart of skyscrapers" by architectural critic Paul Goldberger in 1979, the Woolworth Building is shown in this unusual view from the back (or west), next to the neighboring Transportation Building (right). Designed as the elegant corporate headquarters for Frank Winfield Woolworth's empire of five-and-dime stores, its neo-Gothic style also prompted the sobriquet "Cathedral of Commerce."

99. (FAR RIGHT)

New York, Woolworth Building

1928

Hiroshi Yoshida (Japanese, 1876–1950)
Color woodcut

Celebrated for designing color woodcuts that synthesized a traditional Japanese *ukiyo-e* printmaking aesthetic with a Western style of landscape, Hiroshi Yoshida created more than 250 prints (many were destroyed in the great Tokyo earthquake of 1922) depicting Mount Fuji and the Inland Sea, and scenic wonders such as the Taj Mahal and the Grand Canyon. This print appears to be the only one he made of New York City. It was executed after his third visit to the United States between 1923 and 1925, which included stops in Detroit, Boston, and Philadelphia, as well as Manhattan.

The intimate scale of this subtly colored, lyrical view of the Woolworth Building belies the fact that at the time this print was made it was the tallest building in the world. Its aspiring height, distinctive profile, stepped form, and corporate symbolism would serve as models for skyscraper design in the decade that followed.

100.

The Curving Canyon, New York

1929

Samuel Chamberlain (1895–1975)
Drypoint on paper verdâtre

After studying architecture at the Massachusetts Institute of Technology and then continuing his studies abroad, Samuel Chamberlain decided to specialize in architectural rendering for architectural firms. He supplemented his income by teaching architectural drafting and graphic arts. After creating his first print in 1925, he soon became recognized for the extraordinary linear exactitude of his prints, which resulted in nearly photographic representations of buildings. His work was also acclaimed for its exceptional quality, derived from finely nuanced inkings and carefully selected paper.

All of these distinguishing characteristics are present in this exceptional print featuring the twenty-four–story Cotton Exchange Building, which looms above the narrow confines of Williams Street. Designed by Donn Barber in 1923, the building housed the commodities market founded in 1870 by various cotton merchants (including Southerners such as the Lehman brothers) who had dominated the cotton export business prior to the Civil War. Chamberlain's intimate view dramatically contrasts this building, caught in the sunlight, with others cloaked in deep shadow, such as the C. P. H. Gilbert–designed houses (1903–08) barely discernable to the right of center, with their stepped gables recalling early New Amsterdam dwellings.

91/100   Samuel Chamberlain

THE CURVING CANYON — NEW YORK

101.

Roaring Forties, New York

1929

William C. McNulty (1889–1963)
Etching with drypoint

This aerial view of Times Square looking north from a high-rise (probably on 42nd Street) shows the bustling intersection of Broadway and Seventh Avenue. A *New York Times* reviewer remarked on March 23, 1930 that what William C. McNulty had selectively included in this print "comes closer to being what you unselectively see as you come into this bewildering square and closer still to what you feel." With the passage of time and an increase in traffic within New York City, this crossroads has only become more bewildering. Once the late-nineteenth–century home of horse stables and carriage shops, today it forms the heart of the city's entertainment and tourism industries.

Roaring Forties N.Y. 1929.   Wm C McNulty imp.

102.

The Great White Way Looking toward Times Square from 49th Street

1931

Anton Schutz
(American, born Germany, 1894–1977; to U.S. 1924)
Etching and aquatint

Among Anton Schutz's best prints, this splendid night view shows the dazzling marquees and glowing signs that earned this part of Broadway its reputation as the "The Great White Way." (The moniker was reputedly coined in 1901 by O. J. Oude, who created much of the advertising that appeared on Broadway's plethora of billboards and electric signs.) The pulsating center of American theater, vaudeville, popular music, and moving picture industries in the 1930s, the street is alive with vehicles and pedestrians.

The first theater opened in this area in 1893. In 1928, the first moving electric sign appeared atop *The New York Times* building (after which Times Square was named).

The Great White Way looking towards Times Square from 43rd St. 1931

103.

Lower Manhattan Seen from
2 Montague Terrace, Brooklyn Heights

1931

Anton Schutz
(American, born Germany, 1894–1977; to U.S. 1924)
Color aquatint on yellow tinted paper

Anton Schutz's view of Lower Manhattan provides a startling twentieth-century counterpart to those of William Burgis (plate 3) and William Bennett (after John William Hill, plate 20). Taken from approximately the same vantage point in Brooklyn, it dramatically underscores the success with which the skyscraper had come to dominate the area of earliest settlement in New York. This dramatic night scene printed on yellow paper is exceptional in Schutz's work and, indeed, in city views of the period.

Lower Manhattan seen from Montague Terrace, 1931   A. Schmidt

104.

Plaza Lights, Looking Downtown from
Central Park and 65th Street

1931

Anton Schutz
(American, born Germany, 1894–1977; to U.S. 1924)
Aquatint on turquoise paper

Plaza Lights, looking down town from Central Park and 65th Street, 1931   imp. [signature]

105. (RIGHT)

Docks, Fulton Market

William C. McNulty (1889–1963)
Drypoint

106. (FAR RIGHT)

Under Brooklyn Bridge

1931

William C. McNulty (1889–1963)
Drypoint

Under Brooklyn Bridge   Wm C Welsh

107. (FAR RIGHT)

New York Skyline

1932

Ernest Fiene (1894–1965)
Lithograph, printed by George C. Miller

108. (RIGHT)

Financial Towers, Downtown New York between Wall Street and Old Slip

1935

Ernest D. Roth
(American, born Germany, 1879–1964; to U.S. 1882)
Etching

109.

Pylons, Hudson Bridge, View Between 176–177 Streets, New York City

November 17, 1928

Frederick K. Detwiller (1882–1953)
Etching and aquatint with hand coloring

After decades of deliberation about where and how to build a bridge over the Hudson River, in January 1926 the Port Authority selected Cass Gilbert to design a span extending from West 178th Street and Fort Washington Avenue to Fort Lee, New Jersey. The architect of many important New York buildings—notably the beaux-arts U.S. Customs House (1901–07) and the neo-Gothic Woolworth Building (1911–13; plates 98, 99)—Gilbert experimented with a new venture here in taking on the complex bridge commission. He was to design the granite cladding of the towers, the anchoring piers, the approaches, toll booths, and numerous other elements.

Budgetary factors and the public's changing aesthetic taste, as well as considerations regarding how well the bridge would blend into its Riverside Drive and Palisades surroundings, strongly impacted Gilbert's final design, which was never implemented. Othmar H. Ammann, the visionary Swiss-born chief engineer for the bridge, instead came to play a vital role in overseeing the bridge's design.

As the longest suspension bridge in the world at that time, the Hudson Bridge (now known as the George Washington Bridge) attracted considerable public attention, including that of numerous printmakers who charted its construction.

Frederick K. Detwiller's forcefully drawn, bitten and inked intaglio presents the steel grid work of the pylons. Gilbert's plan called for sheathing each pylon in stone, but because of the Great Depression's impact on the project's budget, Ammann decided to keep the skeletal framework exposed. Although dictated by financial necessity, this decision actually resulted in a more daring design—one that epitomized the power and unornamented beauty of the modern machine age.

© Plate 20 Imp 29 - Pylons Hudson Bridge - View between 176-177 St. N.Y.C. — R. Detwiller Nov 17 1928

110. (RIGHT)

Power, Washington Bridge,
New York City

1931

Gottlob L. Briem
(American, born Germany, 1899–1972; to U.S. 1926)
Etching

111. (FAR RIGHT)

Tower under Construction,
Washington Bridge

1931

Gottlob L. Briem
(American, born Germany, 1899–1972; to U.S. 1926)
Etching

Gottlob Briem, the son of a custom piano manufacturer in Germany, first came to New York in 1926 to learn American methods of piano construction. Instead, he focused his energies on his evening classes at the Grand Central School of Art, where he studied with Arshile Gorky. After deciding to give up a lucrative career in his father's business, he remained in the city to eke out a living as an artist. Between 1930 and 1942 (when he moved to Vermont), he created a number of drawings, paintings, and etchings that were much admired by his peers.

A remarkable series of etchings signaling the artist's fascination with the technical aspects of the George Washington Bridge—its building materials, masonry work, and structural engineering—were produced in 1931. In these two prints, the underside of the bridge's deck and a massive tower that supports its broad sweep of cable wire are rendered in exquisite detail.

Tower. Washington Bridge N.Y.C.   100/12 Imp.   E.L. Bacon '32.

Tower under construction   100/0   G.L. Bacon imp.
Washington Bridge 1931

112.

George Washington Bridge Showing Manhattan Approaches

1932

Anton Schutz
(American, born Germany, 1894–1977; to U.S. 1924)
Etching, second state

On October 24, 1931, the George Washington Bridge opened to traffic. Anton Schutz's print shows the graceful silhouette of the newly completed 3,502-foot bridge supported by four suspended cables. Manufactured by John A. Roebling's Sons in Trenton, the cables were one-and-a-half–times stronger than the cables supporting the Brooklyn Bridge.

Second State.   C. J. Allen

113.

Towers of Manhattan, 42nd Street Group

1930

Albert Flanagan (1886–1969)
Etching

The distinctive, solitary spire in this midtown view belongs to the Chrysler Building, the stunning Art Deco masterpiece by architect William Van Alen (1928–30). The building was personally financed by automobile magnate Walter P. Chrysler to promote his corporation's dedication to quality design. After the 1929 stock market crash, skyscraper architects rarely dared the exuberance broadcast by the Chrysler's tiered sunburst spire and flamboyant ornamentation.

Albert Flanagan's view documents the skyscraper just after its completion. Although surrounded today by other high-rises, the Chrysler Building, remains a shimmering zenith in the New York skyline.

114.

Manhattan Minarets

1931

Walter Tittle (1883–1966)
Drypoint

This dramatic nocturne was made by the portraitist Walter Tittle shortly after the completion of the New York Central (now Helmsley), Chrysler, and Chanin buildings (left, center, and right). It conveys the enchantment and wonder that viewers experienced when beholding the illuminated crowns of this regal trio—the first high-rise commercial buildings to adorn midtown Manhattan. The "minarets" of Tittle's title evokes the traditional towers that similarly dominated their surroundings centuries before the advent of the modern skyscraper.

115.

Empire State Building

1931

Werner Drewes
(American, born Germany, 1899–1985; to U.S. 1930)
Drypoint and roulette

After studying at the Bauhaus with Johannes Itten, Paul Klee, and Wassily Kandinsky, Werner Drewes immigrated to the United States in 1930, where he immediately applied his modernist sensibility to making prints of New York City. One of only a few impressions Drewes made of this print before the plate was destroyed, this rare proof depicts the Empire State Building just as its upper stories were completed. With a few well-placed marks and the white of the paper, Drewes evoked the building's soaring verticality. A dark, low-rise church in the foreground contrasts dramatically with the new light-reflecting architecture, its deep, charred-black inking prompting the print's usual title, *Empire State Building with Church Ruin.* "Ruin" is, in fact, a misnomer, since Drewes's experimental approach took a bit of artistic license with the depiction of the Little Church around the Corner (plate 78), which was probably darkened by shadow rather than by disaster. Drewes soon became a leading American abstract artist, who, in the course of his prolific career, made nearly 750 prints and over one thousand paintings.

Pr. V   w. Drewes - 1931

116.

The Empire State Building Seen from 29th Street and the Hotel Seville

[also called *The Old and the New*] 1932

Anton Schutz
(German, 1894–1977; to U.S. in 1924)
Etching, second state of first proof

Heralded as the eighth wonder of the world when it opened on May 1, 1931, the 1,250-foot-tall Empire State Building (Shreve, Lamb & Harmon, architects, 1930–31) represented an architectural, engineering, labor, and business triumph in the midst of the Great Depression. Planned by former General Motors executive John J. Raskob with industrialist Pierre du Pont, and headed by former New York governor Al Smith, this speculative office building began the transformation of Fifth Avenue in the 30s from a residential neighborhood into a commercial center.

Built economically and in record time, the Empire State Building went up at an astonishing rate of four floors per week due to the then-unprecedented use of prefabricated building components. Its granite- and limestone–clad steel-frame structure was decorated with aluminum panels and nickel detailing. Its massing and stepped profile—a response to the city's 1916 zoning laws—served as distinguished paradigms of skyscraper design until 1950. Surpassed as the world's tallest building with the 1972 completion of the World Trade Center, the building continues to provide visitors with one of the most spectacular views of the city from its 102nd-floor observation deck.

Anton Schutz's view of this celebrated architectural achievement shows the rooftop of the Little Church Around the Corner (plate 78) in the foreground, hence his alternate title *The Old and the New*. His inclusion of a formation of airplanes in the composition was intended as an indicator of scale. Prior to September 11, 2001, the planes might have reminded viewers of the memorable scene in the 1933 film classic *King Kong*; to post 9/11 viewers, however, the proximity of the planes to the lone tower has ominous associations.

Second State first proof — The Empire State Building seen from 29th Street
and Hotel Seville, showing Little Church Around the Corner.

117. (RIGHT)

Manhattan Forum

c. 1931–32

Chester B. Price (1885–1962)
Drypoint

The elevated plaza in front of the Fifth Avenue facade of the New York Public Library (1898–1911) provides the setting for this view by Chester Price. Here, before Carrère and Hastings's classically inspired "temple of knowledge," groups of men engage in discussion, just as their predecessors did at the forum in ancient Rome. In the distance, the Empire State Building rises like a beacon, signaling the triumph of modern civilization.

118. (FAR RIGHT)

Modern New York

1933

William Meyerowitz
(American, born Russia, 1887–1981; to U.S. 1908)
Etching

William Meyerowitz, who immigrated to New York City from the Ukraine in 1908, was jolted into pursuing a bolder, less-traditional style of art by the powerful cubist and abstract works he saw at the ground-breaking 1913 Armory Show. Although he was less artistically adventurous than his friends John Marin, William Zorach, and Mark Rothko, in the 1920s and 1930s he created a number of modernist cityscapes with fragmented forms, including this composite view of midtown buildings surrounding the twin Gothic-revival steeples of St. Patrick's Cathedral (James Renwick, Jr., architect, 1858–79; towers, 1888).

While not literally representational, Meyerowitz's print conveys the energy of the 1930s, when new buildings sprouted skyward, thereby dwarfing the cathedral's previously dominant spires. By placing the revered seat of the Catholic Archdiocese of New York at the center of the image, however, the artist emphasized the enduring grace and monumentality of the building, an important American example of traditional European-inspired ecclesiastical architecture.

119. (RIGHT)

Central Synagogue
[formerly Congregation Ahawath Chesed],
Lexington Avenue at 55th Street

1931

Mortimer Borne
(American, born Poland, 1902–1987; to U.S. 1916)
Drypoint

This Moorish-revival–style synagogue (1870–72) modeled on one in Budapest is home to the oldest Reform congregation (founded 1846 by Bohemian immigrants) in continuous service in New York City. Its German-born architect, Henry Fernbach, who studied in Berlin before immigrating to this country in 1855, was one of the first Jewish architects to practice in the United States. In 1975, this synagogue—skillfully recorded here by the Polish-born printmaker Mortimer Borne—was designated a National Historic Landmark.

120. (FAR RIGHT)

Temple Emanu-El from Central Park

1931

Mortimer Borne
(American, born Poland, 1902–1987; to U.S. 1916)
Drypoint

Mortimer Borne depicted the Temple Emanu-El, as seen through the foliage of Central Park, shortly after it was completed in 1929. It was designed by Robert D. Kohn, Charles Butler, and Clarence Stein in a distinctive Romanesque-revival style.

2

Mortimer Borne. imp

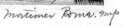

Mortimer Borne imp.

121.

Subway

1932

James Penney (1910–1982)
Lithograph

New York City commuters will appreciate the humor of this print, which captures the crush of passengers on a subway car. James Penney made the viewer the reader of the *Daily Mirror*, which sports the eye-popping headline "'Not My Baby' says Roosev[elt]."

Penney executed this print while attending the Art Students League; among his teachers were Thomas Hart Benton, George Grosz, and John Sloan—all of whom masterfully observed human behavior in order to graphically depict the anecdotal aspects of daily life.

Numerous American artists have made the subway the subject of their art. Every ride presents a fascinating opportunity to study individual gestures and styles of dress, as well as the different economic, cultural, and racial microcosms within the city.

"Subway"   3/10   Jerome Brewly 1932

122.

Hooverville (on Hudson)

1934

Mortimer Borne
(American, born Poland, 1902–1987; to U.S. 1916)
Drypoint

Since the seventeenth century,
churches, charities, social workers,
and civic leaders have attempted to
take appropriate measures to improve
the conditions of the poor and the
homeless in New York City. Yet,
during the nineteenth century,
shantytowns sprouted up in various
parts of the city, particularly on the
West Side. During the Depression,
these shantytowns (known as
"Hoovervilles," after President
Herbert Hoover) numbered about
twenty and housed approximately
two thousand (mostly male) residents.
The largest was "Hard Luck Town,"
a Hooverville at 9th Street and the
East River, which accommodated
450 residents in 1933.

123.

Queensboro Bridge, Manhattan, from Welfare Island

1935

Ernest D. Roth
(American, born Germany, 1879–1964; to U.S. 1882)
Etching

Ernest D. Roth's print features the Queensboro Bridge (Henry Hornbostel, architect, and Gustav Lindenthal, engineer, 1901–08). A major feat of cantilever construction, with its double deck and ornate ironwork the bridge has become a city landmark. It was the first bridge to cross the East River connecting Manhattan (at 59th Street) and Queens, with Welfare Island (as Roosevelt Island was then called) providing anchorage for a pier at mid-span.

Queensboro Bridge—Manhattan—

E. D. Roth 1935

124.

Old Greenwich Village

1928

Mabel Dwight (1876–1955)
Lithograph

An heir to the lithography tradition of the great nineteenth-century French caricaturist Honoré Daumier, Mabel Dwight created satirical prints acclaimed for their masterful portrayal of the *comédie humaine*. Armed with a sketchbook, she made New York City her happy hunting ground. In 1928—the year this print was made—she had her first solo exhibition at New York's Weyhe Gallery; by 1936, she was considered among the best living American printmakers.

At various times, Dwight resided in Greenwich Village. Her 1928 print presents the area as quaint and homey, filled with mothers pushing baby carriages, children playing safely on cobblestone streets, and laundry drying on the line. Small wooden houses—replaced by brick and stone buildings in other areas of New York City in the nineteenth century—preserve the picturesque rural character of what was once a country hamlet.

As the city expanded to encompass Greenwich Village, the population of the former farming community grew, swelled by an influx of freed slaves and, later, Italian immigrants. But slow to modernize, the area retained its village character into the twentieth century.

Mabel Dwight

125.

Jefferson Market Clock

c. 1933–37 (?)

Frank [Francis Joseph] Hanley (1913–?)
Linocut

This print, with its simplified, unmodulated areas of black, evokes the charming architecture of the West Village. It features the Jefferson Market Courthouse (Frederick Withers and Calvert Vaux, architects, 1874–77), located on Sixth Avenue at West 10th Street and named after the meat and produce market that formerly occupied the site. An extraordinary example of High Victorian architecture more characteristic of London than New York, the building's distinctive bell and clock tower (with space for a firewatch) presides over a panoply of turrets and gables. While some 1870s critics worried that the lowliest of criminals would be housed in one of the city's most ornate buildings, others felt that the secular building decorated in such an exalted ecclesiastical style might help reform its vagrant and wayward detainees and further benefit the course of justice.

In 1960, local residents helped to designate the Jefferson Market Courthouse a historic landmark. It is now used as a branch of the New York Public Library.

Jefferson Market Clock   Frank Hanley

126.

Sweet Potato Man

1936

Lou Barlow (born 1908)
Wood engraving, stamped "New York City WPA Art Project"

During the Great Depression of the 1930s, the Works Progress Administration (WPA), which provided jobs for unemployed artists, writers, musicians, and actors, was among the various agencies established under President Franklin D. Roosevelt's administration to ameliorate the public's economic plight. Throughout the country, more than five thousand artists were engaged to create murals, easel paintings, sculptures, and prints to decorate various public buildings, from schools to post offices to government bureaus. The New York workshop of the WPA's Graphic Arts Division employed fifty artists, who were furnished with supplies and access to professional printers, in addition to being paid a regular salary. The art that resulted was distinctly American in character, reflecting aspects of national life and brimming with undaunted ingenuity.

Street vendors have existed in New York City since colonial times. In the nineteenth century, as today, immigrants who had no other means of steady income gained their livelihood as street peddlers. During the Depression, sidewalk vendors offering affordable food and wares were just as prevalent. Lou Barlow's print depicts a typical curbside scene, which serves as a telling document of the WPA era.

Sweet Potato Man   Lou Barlow

127. (RIGHT)

The Orange Cart, Orchard Street, New York

1934

William C. McNulty (1889–1963)
Etching

128. (FAR RIGHT)

Marketing on Avenue A

1936

Betty Waldo Parish
(American, born Germany, 1910–1986; to U.S. c. 1926)
Etching

"Marketing on Avenue A.   Betty Waldo Parish

Etching on copper   Spring 1936

129.

The Fountain, Central Park, New York

1933

Albert E. Flanagan (1886–1969)
Drypoint

Probably the most important American water feature created in the nineteenth century, Bethesda Fountain was designed and realized in the heart of Central Park by architects Calvert Vaux and Jacob Wrey Mould in 1873. The statue that adorns it, shown in Albert Flanagan's print as a winged silhouette, is the *Angel of Waters* by the little-known sculptor Emma Stebbins. The fountain's name was inspired by a biblical passage about an angel who touches the water of Jerusalem's Bethesda Pool, thereby giving it curative power. Designed for a park that was envisioned as a naturalistic retreat, where city dwellers could become reinvigorated, the fountain's symbolism is apt.

130. (RIGHT)

The Eternal Light, New York

1935

Julius F. Gayler (1872–1948)
Etching and aquatint

131. (FAR RIGHT)

Eternal Light, Madison Square

1937

Edith Nankivell (1896–1984)
Etching and aquatint

The Eternal Light Memorial, a 120-foot flagpole topped by a multifaceted star, was designed by sculptor Paul Bartlett and architect Thomas Hastings to commemorate soldiers who died in France during World War I. Installed in Madison Square Park in June 1924, it remained until 1973, when it was replaced with an updated version. Both Julius F. Gayler (an accomplished print artist as well as architect, who worked with Carrère and Hastings before establishing his own firm) and Edith Nankivell (who, like her father, the artist Frank Nankivell, depicted many New York scenes) expertly used the rich black possible with the aquatint technique to evoke a dramatic night scene. The park is illuminated by the astral glow of the memorial, the ghostly presence of the Flatiron Building visible in the background.

132.

Saint Paul's Chapel,

New York

1939

Julius F. Gayler (1872–1948)
Etching and aquatint, first state

Saint Paul's Church
New York 1938   First State   Aylin T Tayler

133.

Library of Columbia University, New York City

1933

Ernest D. Roth
(American, born Germany, 1879–1964; to U.S. 1882)
Etching

Founded in 1754, Columbia University is the oldest educational institution in New York City and among the oldest in the country. In 1894, in preparation for the relocation of its main campus from midtown to Morningside Heights, university leaders contracted the architectural firm of McKim, Mead & White to create the new master plan. Instead of designing in the Gothic-revival style that characterized many other nineteenth-century American campuses, the École de Beaux-Arts–trained architects selected classical precedents for the earliest buildings constructed, which were built on axis with 116th Street between Broadway and Amsterdam Avenue.

Raised above an expansive plaza, the grand, domed Low Memorial Library forms the centerpiece of the campus plan. Seth Low, who was Columbia's president from 1890 to 1901 and thus oversaw the university's move, gave the funding for the new library building in memory of his father, Abiel Abbot Low (1811–1893), a merchant specializing in the trade of Chinese teas. Today, the library still symbolizes the heart of the (much-expanded) campus.

Library of Columbia University

Ernest D. Roth 1933

134.

Chance Meeting

1940–41

Martin Lewis
(American, born Australia, 1882–1962; to U.S. 1900)
Drypoint

Although he began as a commercial artist, Martin Lewis became one of New York City's technically finest printmakers, first learning the practice in 1915. He particularly excelled in creating dramatic night scenes of the city featuring striking contrasts of light and deep shadow as well as silhouettes and figures sharply defined by beams of illumination.

This view of a typical neighborhood storefront, with the 7Up sign displayed as prominently as the nearby flag, depicts a specific episode that city dwellers recognize as a common urban occurrence: a random encounter between two people at any given moment of the day.

135.

Chinatown, Doyers Street

1940

Mortimer Borne
(American, born Poland, 1902–1987; to U.S. 1916)
Drypoint

While sitting on the sidewalk and without creating any preliminary sketches, the artist drew this image directly onto a copper plate. Using a diamond-pointed drypoint needle, he recorded the picturesque appearance of a sparsely peopled Doyers Street in Chinatown. Due to the nature of the printmaking process, the words on restaurant and shop signs, executed correctly on the plate, are reversed in the finished print.

Although Chinatown had grown during the twentieth century, the Chinese still constituted a small minority within a city that numbered over 7.4 million. In 1943, after the United States and China became allies in World War II, the Chinese Exclusion Act was repealed, thereby permitting Chinese immigrants to become citizens; yet, at the same time, the quota for immigrants from China was only 105 persons per year.

Doyers St.   Mortimer Borne '40 imp

136. (RIGHT)

Henry Street, Brooklyn Heights

1941

Mortimer Borne
(American, born Poland, 1902–1987; to U.S. 1916)
Drypoint

137. (FAR RIGHT)

A Day in the Park

c. 1942

Ralph Fabri
(American, born Hungary, 1894–1975; to U.S. 1921)
Etching with drypoint

After studying architecture in Budapest, Ralph Fabri emigrated to New York. There, the prolific printmaker became a noted teacher at such area art schools as the Parsons School of Design and the National Academy of Design. During World War II, his prints of fighter planes, search lights, legions of fighters, and graves hauntingly conveyed the horrors of combat and other nightmarish visions.

After 1942, he actively participated in Artists for Victory, Inc., a national nonprofit organization inspired by President Franklin D. Roosevelt's "Four Freedoms" speech to support the United States war effort. Members provided visual arts services for local communities, government agencies, industry, and business. Fabri's print of New Yorkers enjoying a variety of recreational pastimes in Central Park, under a rainbow of airplanes arching over the city, was probably created to inspire patriotism and community well-being during wartime.

a Day in the Park   4/50   Ralph Fabri, S.A.E.

138. (RIGHT)

East of Gramercy

(22nd Street between Third and Second Avenues)

1950–51

Betty Waldo Parish
(American, born Germany, 1910–1986; to U.S. c. 1926)
Wood engraving

139. (FAR RIGHT)

Encroachment of a City—

Lower Battery Park

1946–52

Betty Waldo Parish
(American, born Germany, 1910–1986; to U.S. c. 1926)
Engraving

3/19

sketch made directly on block.
June July - 1950. Released Dec 1951
Wood Engraving

East of Gramercy

Purchased by Pennell Fund
for Library of Congress - 1951 Also in Metropolitan Museum - Arms Memorial

Betty Waldo Parish

22 St. between 3rd and 2nd Aves

$/25

Lower Battery Park.
Sketch made Fall of 1946.
Prints released November 1952.

Encroachment of a City

Engraving in copper. Some small etching remaining

Betty Waldo Parish

140.

Little Singer Building

1971

Richard Haas (born 1936)
Etching

Richard Haas's remarkable architectural elevations serve as portraits of buildings. This prolific printmaker, tromp l'oeil architectural muralist, and painter here uses the crisp linearity possible in etching to depict the ornate facade of the Little Singer Building in SoHo. Designed by architect Ernest Flagg in 1904 to house the Singer Manufacturing Company, its unusual L-shaped plan wraps around a corner building, resulting in two distinct facades—one on Broadway, and one on Prince Street. Among the most charming of the neighborhood's cast-iron buildings, its delicate metal and glass "skin" anticipates the curtain wall of the modern skyscraper.

141. (RIGHT)

Flatiron Building

1973

Richard Haas (born 1936)
Etching

142. (FAR RIGHT)

Flatiron

1993

[Arthur] John Harris (born 1959)
Etching

When it was completed in 1902, the twenty-one story Fuller Building designed by Daniel H. Burnham & Company signaled the beginning of New York City's skyscraper era. Unprecedented in height, with Renaissance-revival–style decorative cladding covering its then-innovative steel structure, it reigned as the city's tallest structure until the completion of the Woolworth Building in 1913 (plates 98, 99). The structure's form was dictated by its triangular footprint, created by the intersection of Fifth Avenue and Broadway at 23rd Street. Only six feet wide at its tip, the wedge-shaped high-rise soon acquired the nickname the "Flatiron Building" after the household appliance it so resembled.

These two large, late twentieth-century prints recorded this singular, now-beloved architectural landmark from different perspectives. Richard Haas's precisely delineated rendering presented the Flatiron straight on, as viewed from the north. His print emphasized the building's immobility—a condition that ran contrary to the belief held by early skeptics that the thin building would easily topple in high winds. His print also conveyed the monumental scale of the Flatiron in relation to its contemporary neighbors.

In contrast, John Harris's oblique view, composed from ground level looking upward, silhouetted the building against the "sky" of the unprinted paper. His print distorted the building's unusual shape, emphasizing the pedestrian's optical reality rather than the building's spatial reality. Leaving behind the typical tasks of documenting structural details, a sense of scale, and context (as Haas's print does), Harris's print, with its dense network of cross-hatching, suggested the building's rusticated surface and evoked its material presence.

143.

Rising Sun

1977

Richard Sloat (born 1945)
Aquatint

Richard Sloat shows the World Trade Center from his Lower East Side neighborhood looking west (although due to the printmaking process, what is actually on the right is depicted on the left, and vice versa). The artist remarked about this print in 2004:

> It took some time to get to love this architectural leviathan, but by its simple majesty of form, its changing moods of light during the day and its ever burning beacon in the night, it won a place in our hearts. Rising Sun *reflects the energy of the city rising, watched over by the beneficences of the World Trade Center. Now...something is always missing in the sky, [there is] a blank space in our heart.*

The World Trade Center (Minoru Yamasaki and Emery Roth & Sons, architects, 1972 and 1973) was designed and constructed in an era that saw rockets launched into outer space and skyscrapers climb to heights never before achieved by built structures. In a society where "bigger is better," the World Trade Center (WTC) led the way as the largest commercial complex in the world. In terms of height, however, its fraternal-twin towers' tenure as the tallest buildings in the world was short-lived: the WTC was superceded by Chicago's Sears Tower in 1974.

Conceived as a way to modernize Lower Manhattan and to reposition it as an international business center, the WTC was designed as a monument to capitalism's success. Its immense, gleaming verticality attracted global attention as well as stimulated tourism as a unique city landmark—roles that prompted devastating tragedy in 2001.

Rather than looking at the WTC, the public preferred to be inside the towers looking out at the amazing panoramic view they provided. As Sloat's statement implies, local inhabitants were initially reluctant to accept the new colossus in their midst; gradually, however, the WTC became a "natural" element in the city's topography.

144.
White Street

1977

Alan Petrulis (born 1954)
Etching

Alan Petrulis discovers artistic interest in documenting what some viewers might dismiss as too ordinary a neighborhood to merit graphic depiction. Yet it is precisely his focus on aspects of the everyday built environment, of specific sites captured at particular times, that makes the viewer notice the characteristic cacophony of signage, awnings, and vernacular structures that clutter many contemporary New York streetscapes. This typical Lower Manhattan scene with the World Trade Center towers in the background records how their giant scale and minimalist design—so alien in the first years of their existence— became incorporated into the cityscape that evolved around them. Pedestrians soon became accustomed to confirming their orientation on the city's streets with a glance at the twin towers, which loomed above all other buildings.

30/100   White Street   Alan Petrulis

145. (RIGHT)

Old Brownstones,
New York

c. 1983

Lawrence Nelson Wilbur (1897–1988)
Drypoint

146. (FAR RIGHT)

Subterraneans X,
Spring Street

1985

Max Ferguson (born 1959)
Etching

McFerrin 1985

147.

Bronx Crossing

1991

William Behnken (born 1943)
Aquatint

William Behnken, whose virtuosity in aquatint creates tones of black that look like mezzotint, specializes in still-life compositions and night scenes featuring his west Bronx neighborhood of Kingsbridge. This realistic view shows the elevated train at 238th Street and Broadway.

A dedicated graphic artist who has steadily exhibited since 1971, Behnken also teaches art history and studio classes at the City College of New York as well as printmaking classes at the Art Students League.

148.

FDR Drive

1993

Craig McPherson (born 1948)
Mezzotint

The biggest challenge for print artists is printing black tones to evoke the nuances of night and shadows. Craig McPherson—a contemporary painter who is also a master at printing a spectrum of blacks—works in mezzotint because it is the best printmaking technique to achieve a range of light tones and soft half-darks. A native of Kansas, McPherson came to New York City in 1975; shortly thereafter, he taught himself the exacting mezzotint technique by creating reproductive plates of flowers. His trilogy of grand night cityscapes includes his most famous mezzotint, *Yankee Stadium at Night* (1983), featuring the atmospheric glow of the stadium's lights; *Girders* (1986), a panoramic vista from the artist's former Washington Heights studio; and this print, of FDR Drive.

The East River Drive, which runs along the eastern edge of Manhattan, is better known as the FDR Drive (for Franklin Delano Roosevelt). Built at the direction of powerful city planner Robert Moses during the administration of Mayor Fiorello La Guardia, it opened in 1942. McPherson's view shows the road under the bridge at 81st Street as seen looking south from Carl Schurz Park; part of the Queensboro Bridge appears in the distance.

This tour-de-force of mezzotint printmaking evokes a rainy night. McPherson's remarkable observations and technical skill captured the light reflecting off the wet pavement (cleverly contrasted with reflections on the surface of the East River) as well as rain caught in the glow of the streetlights.

149.
Early Thaw

1996

Art Werger (born 1955)
Mezzotint

Based on a photograph of a picturesque stretch of sidewalk flanking
Central Park, Art Werger's print
expertly translates a captivating
tapestry of textures and tonalities on
melting snow, puddles, and pavement
into a compelling mezzotint.

150.

Walk Down St. Mark's

1994

Richard Sloat (born 1945)
Etching and aquatint

This view vividly captures what the artist terms "the hustle and bustle of the night life" on St. Mark's Place (8th Street), a lively East Village street named for the nearby church of St. Mark's-in-the-Bowery. Because of the area's affordable housing, many intellectuals, writers, poets, artists, and musicians moved there starting in the 1960s; the neighborhood developed into a tolerant, multiethnic community known for its bookstores, coffee houses, eateries, bars, jazz clubs, cutting-edge performance theaters, and punk rockers. It is a neighborhood that has dealt with radical politics, gay rights, hippies, homelessness, and drugs, and through it all has continued to thrive.

Richard Sloat, whose home with his wife, artist Su-Li Hung, is in the East Village, created this print to reflect his fascination with the people who steadily stream down St. Mark's Place in a "seemingly endless parade. . . of humanity."

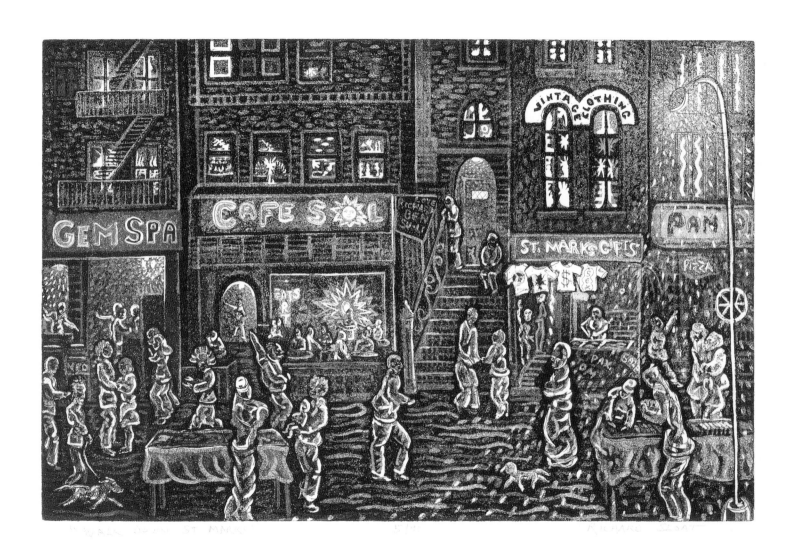

151. (RIGHT)

Daybreak

1997

Art Werger (born 1955)
Mezzotint

152. (FAR RIGHT)

Evening Rain

1998

Daniel Hauben (born 1956)
Color intaglio

153. (TOP)

From Silver Lake

1999

Bill Murphy (born 1952)
Etching

154. (FAR RIGHT)

Sunset Skyline

[View from the Artist's Studio in Astoria, Queens]

1997

Steven Walker (born 1955)
Two-color aquatint (with surface roll)

Staten Island places and vistas inspire the art of Bill Murphy, a lifelong inhabitant of the island. This print shows a view of distant Manhattan, with the World Trade Center as the prominent landmark, as seen from the artist's Silver Lake neighborhood. One in a long lineage of artists who regularly document familiar surroundings, Murphy works in a wiry, linear style that was more prevalent from the 1880s to the mid-twentieth century than it is today. His prints consciously revive the graphic style forged by great American etchers of the past, such as Thomas Moran, Frederick Leo Hunter, Edward Hopper, and Martin Lewis.

27/70 SUNSET SKYLINE   S. Walker

155.
World Trade View

1995

Emily Trueblood (born 1942)
Two-color linocut

Emily Trueblood frequently creates
prints in a particularly small size to
encourage intimacy with the
immense scale of the city's urban
panorama. Here, seen from a
building's upper floor, beyond
ubiquitous water tanks and low-rise
buildings, are the World Trade Center
towers. By deliberately cropping out
the top of the buildings, Trueblood
reminds the viewer that a single gaze
could never take in the WTC's full
height. Her print also accentuates the
sharply defined shaft of light and
space in between the trade center's
towers, the void being as palpable a
geometric element as the seemingly
invincible solid structures flanking it.

31/50   World Trade View   Woolfson © '95

156. (BOTTOM)

Broken City

2001

Su-Li Hung
(American, born Taiwan, 1947; to New York 1970)
Color woodcut

157. (RIGHT)

World Trade Center

2001

Su-Li Hung
(American, born Taiwan, 1947; to New York 1970)
Woodcut

Born in a small fishing village in southern Taiwan, Su-Li Hung first came to New York to study art. She became so fascinated by the city's unceasing energy, as well as by its multitextured, multipatterned, interwoven fabric, that she decided to adopt the city as her own. Alternating between woodcut printmaking (combining her heritage of traditional Chinese woodcut styles with a western sensibility) and collage as her primary media, she depicts buildings, streets, neighborhoods, and the kaleidoscopic variety of New York City life.

After the tragic disaster of September 11, 2001—the most catastrophic disaster in the city's history—Hung distilled her feelings in a poem:

Instant dust blows
smoke descends
fire of melting rock
flowers of frozen blood.

She also made several memory images of the World Trade Center to evoke the city's pervasive sense of mourning and disquiet. In one print (plate 157), the former 110-story towers also evoke two monumented steles marking a grave site. In the other (plate 156), a building crumbles behind a pair of rigid, parallel rectangles in pale blue—the unyielding, vestigial "shadows" of the twin towers.

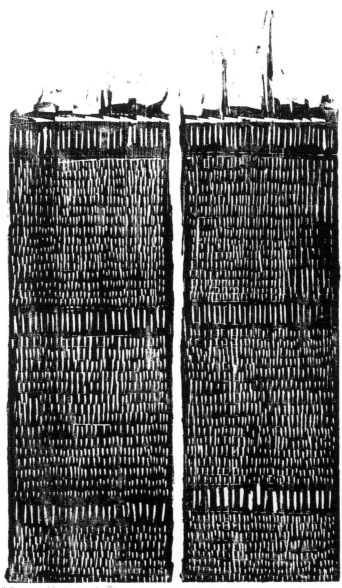

2/50   world trade Center   Su-Li Hung   2001

158.

42nd and 5th [View of New York Public Library]

1998

Martin Levine (born 1945)
Etching and aquatint on chine collé

159.

Parapets

2001

Michael di Cerbo (born 1947)
Etching and aquatint

Every day, multitudes experience New York's skyscrapers from street level, looking upward at the gigantic buildings that line the city's blocks. Michael di Cerbo's asphalt-black print suggests the appearance of all skyscrapers but no specific building, viewed from a "worm's-eye" perspective. A dedicated printmaker and self-described "street prowler," di Cerbo is constantly fueled by the immensity and profusion of New York City's rectilinear monoliths.

New York–based architect and writer Michael Sorkin once commented that the New York skyscraper "occurs at the intersection of greed and grid": the city's skyline resulted more from real estate concerns than from a grand architectural master plan. Di Cerbo's print documents this post-1950 reality of urban evolution, as experienced from the city's sidewalks.

15/70   Parapets   Michael Le B 2001

160.

On Your Mark, Get Set, Go!

2002

Red Grooms (born 1937)
Color lithograph, published by Marlborough Graphics

A native of Nashville, Red Grooms is a sculptor, painter, installation and performance artist, film maker, and printmaker who portrays humanity—particularly the New York variety—with a celebrated brand of irrepressible wit and exuberance. He has lived in New York since 1957.

The subject of this print, created one year after the devastating tragedy of September 11, 2001, is an appropriate acknowledgment of the triumph of the human spirit and of individual achievement exemplified by racers in the New York City Marathon, one of the most important annual city events. His vertigo-producing view looks down on the throng of runners on the Verrazano-Narrows Bridge, the place where the marathon traditionally starts. In the bay, Grooms includes many boats that have congregated to witness the exciting moment when thousands of racers, including wheel chair entrants, commence their journey through the city's diverse neighborhoods. The prominent display of the U.S. flag signals the show of patriotism that, throughout New York City and the rest of the country, was particularly in evidence at the time, as individual and collective displays of solidarity and strength.

The first New York City Marathon took place in Central Park in September 1970; there were 127 starting racers and 55 finishers. Since then, the marathon has expanded beyond Manhattan to include the streets of all five boroughs. In 2002 more than 34,700 runners from around the world participated.

B A T   Red Grooms 2002

161.

Downtown

2003

Karen Whitman (born 1953)
Linocut

In the days, weeks, months, and years after September 11, 2001, the city gradually healed and regained its customary resilience. Karen Whitman's print shows, in a playful way, ordinary aspects of contemporary daily life that persist in the city: ball-playing, dog walking, and street vending; smoke stacks, water tanks, the Brooklyn Bridge, striped crosswalks, a manhole cover, and a dangling traffic light. The print also includes two objects that exemplify people's increased reverence in a post-9/11 era for courage and patriotism: the fire truck alludes to the heroism displayed by firemen during every fire, but spectacularly during September 11; the United States flag (in this image, on the post office building) signals the sense of unity and national pride that were renewed after the harrowing events of that day.

276

162. (RIGHT)

City Signs

[Brooklyn-Queens Expressway]

2003

Michael Pellettieri (born 1943)
Lithograph

163. (FAR RIGHT)

Intersection

[at Queensboro Bridge]

1999–2000

Phyllis Seltzer (born 1928)
Heat transfer print

164.

Attraction (Times Square, New York)

2003

Art Werger (born 1955)
Mezzotint

This extraordinary, skillfully realized, large-scale mezzotint is a composite image, derived from several photographs taken by the artist from various vantage points. Rather than literally depict a single view, Art Werger—inspired by cinematic splicing wizardry—instead re-creates the intense experience of visiting Times Square: the visual cacophony of oversized signs and images that constantly flicker, pan, and pulsate; the ebb and flow of surging crowds; the endless river of taxis and other vehicles; the electrifying jolts of palpable energy. Confident in its role, the area exudes the aura that it truly is the center of the man-made universe. Every minute of every day, countless people are drawn by the all-pervasive attraction of this specific place, where money, power, commerce, glitz, technology, and innovation converge. The square is both destination and urban hub, constantly accommodating visitors while permitting passage through its core.

165.

New York Harbor Composite

2 0 0 3

Yvonne Jacquette (born 1934)
Woodcut

Yvonne Jacquette is the master artist of the aerial view from a contemporary perspective. Her paintings, drawings, and prints present spectacular daytime and nocturnal views of American cities, suburbs, industrial areas, farmland, waterways, and wilderness based on vistas seen from elevated vantage points. Her art is about bringing "intimacy to the vastness" of both cityscapes and the natural landscape.

This print is a view of the southwestern tip of Manhattan, which is roughly (as landfill was added) the site where New York City originated. Almost 350 years later, Jacquette's woodcut nocturne depicts a completely built-up metropolis. Her view shows part of Cass Gilbert's ornate West Street Building (1905–07; left)

from two different perspectives—one closer (as seen from a lower story) than the other. The diminishing tiers, each dramatically underlit, of the hexagonal roof of the Museum of Jewish Heritage (James Stewart Polshek & Partners, architect, 1990) are in the center, close to the waterfront. At the upper left is the Statue of Liberty (plate 72).

Jacquette exploits the woodcut's capabilities for even tonal areas of printed black to suggest a broad expanse of water in the harbor as well as to create the illusion of spatial depth. She uses the white of the paper as accents of light and animates the print with a series of black and white patterns: in addition to illuminated windows, a necklace of lights rings New York Harbor.

This print is related to two of Jacquette's 1998 paintings: *Mixed Heights and Harbor from the World Trade Center II* and a variant *From the World Trade Center, Mixed Heights II*, held in the New-York Historical

Society's collection. Both works conflated her observations made from two different floors of a building that no longer exists in the wake of September 11, 2001.

This print, published in 2003, serves as a memory document of what the artist saw in the past. Yet it also offers an optimistic glimpse of a prospect to come: with the completion of the Freedom Tower—the twenty-first–century reincarnation of the World Trade Center, which will reach even greater heights—a renewed composite view of Lower Manhattan will again be possible.

APPENDIX

Each of the prints illustrated in this book is held in the Department of Prints, Photographs, and Architectural Collections, which is part of the New-York Historical Society Library. This checklist follows the order in which plates appear in the volume, which is primarily chronological, and provides media, dimensions, acquisition information, and major bibliographic references, which may prove useful for readers interested in researching the work further. Information regarding related objects in the society's collections is also provided.

For each entry, the name of the artist, printmaker, printer, and/or publisher is noted when known; in most cases, this information is furnished by the signature or inscription on the print. For titles not provided by the artist, printmaker, or inscription, every effort has been made to confirm the title in the appropriate scholarly reference; in a few instances, the title is based on dealer catalogue listings. Dating for each artist's and printmaker's lifetime activity is based on factual records (e.g. obituaries, public records, and/or business notices) or has been estimated based on what is set out in scholarly publications. The specific dating for each print comes from either the print's inscription or from published references; for undated prints, probable dates are suggested based upon relevant sources (e.g. contemporary newspaper coverage, address directories, business records, advertisements, and/or scholarly publications) associated with the artist, printmaker, printer, or publisher, or associated with the subject depicted. All media and dimensions have been confirmed for this publication by direct examination of each print; dimensions cite height first, then width. Hand-written and imprinted inscriptions that appear on the prints have not been fully transcribed due to limitations of space.

References to publications that treat prints featured in this book are cited in this appendix by author's last name and (as necessary) date of publication, followed by the pertinent catalogue and/or page number; the full citation follows in the selected bibliography. Acquisition credit lines were specifically researched for this publication; when no credit line is listed, this indicates that, in spite of a thorough search, none could be confirmed in time for publication. In some cases, particularly during the nineteenth and early twentieth centuries, prints often entered the society as part of large gifts of library materials and, unless particularly rare, were described only in a general way. Often considered as material to be added to the picture resource files, they were, like reference books, not customarily credited with any donor's name.

M.S.

FRONTISPIECE
NATHANIEL CURRIER (1813–1888)
New York Bay from the Telegraph Station c. 1850
> Hand-colored lithograph, printed and published by
> Nathaniel Currier, 2 Spruce Street, New York
> Image and sheet 8 7/8 x 11 1/2 in.
> Ref: Gale, no. 4822
> Gift of Buffalo and Erie County Historical Society, 1960

PREFACE
W. J. CONDIT, after C. MILBOURNE (active 1793–1816)
The Government House, a 1797 View 1847
> Color lithograph, printed by William Ells, lithographer;
> published by Henry R. Robinson, New York
> Image 13 5/8 x 20 3/8 in.; sheet 19 3/4 x 24 in.
> Ref.: Stokes, vol. 1 (1915), pl. 66, pp. 443–45; cf. Koke, no.
> 1834 (for related watercolor by Milbourne)
> Gift of Mrs. Byam Kirby Stevens, 1915

ACKNOWLEDGMENTS
ERNEST D. ROTH (American, born Germany, 1879–1964; to U.S. 1882)
The New-York Historical Society 1940
> Etching
> Plate 9 x 12 in.; sheet 11 x 15 1/2 in.
> Commissioned by the New-York Historical Society, 1939
> *Society director Alexander J. Wall, Jr.'s letter of December 8, 1939*
> *offered a sum of $350 as reimbursement for the preliminary*
> *sketch (still in the society's collection), plus an additional $50 to*
> *cover the printing of 100 impressions. The artist confirmed the*
> *agreeent in a letter dated on December 11, 1939.*

INTRODUCTION
LOUIS NAGEL & ADAM WEINGÄRTNER, with figures by CARL EMIL DOEPLER, after GEORG CARSTENSEN and CHARLES GILDEMEISTER, architects
New York Crystal Palace for the Exhibition of the Industry of all Nations 1852
> Lithograph with tan tint stone, with selected hand-coloring,
> published by Goupil & Co., 289 Broadway, New York
> Image 17 7/8 x 28 3/4 in.; sheet 24 1/4 x 35 in.
> Gift of Dewitt M. Lockman, 1927

CHARLES P. HUESTIS [misspelled "HEUSTIS" on the print]
Terrific Explosion at the Great Fire in New-York! Dreadful Loss of Life!! July 1845
> Hand-colored lithograph, printed by George Snyder,
> 112 John Street, New York
> Image 11 1/2 x 13 in.; sheet 17 1/4 x 13 3/4 in.
> Purchase via gift of Leonard Milberg, 1987

CATALOGUE

1. Pieter Mortier, publisher (active in Amsterdam,
   c. 1685–1711)
   N. Amsterdam, ou N Iork in Ameriq. c. 1700
   > Colored engraving
   > Image and border 7 3/8 x 9 1/2 in.; sheet 7 3/4 x 10 3/8 in.
   > Ref.: Stokes, vol. 1 (1915), pl. 14–a, pp. 218–19; cf. Koke, no.
   > 2047
   > *Also in the New-York Historical Society's collection is the*
   > *drawing upon which this engraving is based.*

2. GÉRARD JOLLAIN (French, active c. 1660–1683) or
   FRANÇOIS JOLLAIN (French, 1641–1704)
   Nowel Amsterdam en L'Amérique 1672
   > Hand-colored etching and engraving, with inscription in
   > Latin and French
   > Image 12 1/2 x 19 3/4 in.; sheet 14 x 20 in.
   > Ref.: Stokes, vol. 1 (1915), pl. 12, pp. 215–17;
   > Deák (1988), no. 52
   > Purchase, 1951

3. JOHN HARRIS (English, active 1685–1739) after WILLIAM
   BURGIS (English, active in the American colonies
   1716–after 1731)
   A South Prospect of Ye Flourishing City of New York
   in the Province of New York in America [called "The
   Burgis View"] 1717
   > Engraving from four plates on four sheets, issued c. 1719–21
   > Sheet 21 5/8 x 75 5/8 in. (total length; bottom margin trimmed)
   > Ref.: Stokes, vol. 1 (1915), pl. 25, pp. 239–51;
   > Deák (1988), no. 75
   > Gift of Berthold Fernow, c. 1885
   > *Although Stokes, the great scholar of New York City prints,*
   > *once thought that the society's impression of "The Burgis*
   > *View" was unique, following the initial publication of his*
   > *Iconography another impression emerged; it is now in the*
   > *New York Public Library.*

4. JOHN HARRIS (English, active 1685–1739) after WILLIAM
   BURGIS (English, active in the American colonies
   1716–after 1731)
   A South Prospect of Ye Flourishing City of New York
   in the Province of New York in America [called "The
   Bakewell View," showing the city as it appeared in 1717]
   > Engraving from four plates on four sheets, second state,
   > printed and sold by Thomas Bakewell, London, March 25,
   > 1746
   > Sheet 24 x 77 1/4 in.
   > Ref.: Stokes, vol. 1 (1915), pl. 33, pp. 272–74;
   > Deák (1988), no. 76
   > Gift of B. C. Weekes, 1914

5. Attributed to WILLIAM BURGIS (English, active in the
   American colonies 1716–after 1731)
   View of Fort George, New York, from the West 1730–31
   > Hand-colored mezzotint
   > Image 8 3/4 x 12 1/4 in.; sheet (sight)
   > 9 3/4 x 12 1/4 in.
   > Ref.: Shadwell (1969), no. 10
   > Purchase, 1949

6. JOHN CARWITHAM (English, active c. 1723–1741) after
   WILLIAM BURGIS (?) (English, active in the American
   colonies 1716–after 1731)
   A View of Fort George with the City of New York from
   the Southwest [called "The Carwitham View of New
   York"]
   > Hand-colored engraving, printed for Carington Bowles Map
   > & Printseller, at No. 69 in St. Paul's Church Yard, London;
   > published c. 1764
   > Image 11 3/16 x 17 3/4 in.; sheet 12 x 17 7/8 in.
   > Ref.: Stokes, vol. 1 (1915), pl. 31, pp. 267–69;
   > Deák (1988), no. 84; Olds, no. 4
   > Bequest of Irving S. Olds, 1963

7. CHARLES-BALTHAZAR-JULIEN FÉVRET DE SAINT-MÉMIN
   (French, 1770–1852; active in U.S. 1793–1814)
   View of the City of New-York taken from Long Island
   1796
   > Hand-colored etching, first state
   > Image 13 x 18 7/16 in.; sheet 16 5/8 x 21 7/8 in.
   > Ref.: Stokes, vol. 1 (1915), pl. 61, pp. 437–38;
   > Deák (1988), no. 215
   > *The copper plate for this print is also in the society's*
   > *collection.*

8. After CHARLES-BALTHAZAR-JULIEN-FÉVRET DE SAINT-
   MÉMIN (French, 1770–1852; active in U.S. 1793–1814)
   A View of the City of New-York from Brooklyn Heights
   in 1798 by Monsieur C. B. Julien de Saint-Mémin
   with a Pantograph invented by Himself
   > Engraving (on three sheets), published by Matthew Dripps
   > c. 1850 from an original drawing in the possession of
   > J. C. Brevoort Esq. of Brooklyn
   > Sheet (mounted) 4 3/4 x 56 3/4 in.
   > Ref.: Stokes, vol. 3 (1918), pl. 80–a, pp. 541–42;
   > Deák (1988), no. 218
   > Gift of J. Carson Brevoort, 1886

9. JOHN JAMES BARRALET (Irish, c. 1747–1815; active in U.S.
   after 1795) after a sketch by WILLIAM H. (?) MORGAN
   taken on the spot
   Launch of the Steam Frigate Fulton the First *at New*
   York 29th October 1814
   > Engraving, published by Benjamin Tanner,
   > Philadelphia, March 27, 1815
   > Image 10 x 15 in.; sheet 12 3/8 x 15 3/4 in.
   > Ref.: Stokes, vol. 3 (1918), pl. 83–a, pp. 556–57;
   > Deák (1988), no. 289
   > Bequest of Randall J. LeBoeuf, Jr., 1979

10. LOUIS-JULES-FRÉDERIC VILLENEUVE (French, 1796–1842) after JACQUES-GÉRARD MILBERT (French, 1766–1840; visited North America 1815–1823), with figures by VICTOR ADAM (French, 1801–1866)
Interior of New-York, Provost Street and Chapel
1816–23

    Lithograph, from *Itinéraire pittoresque du fleuve Hudson et des parties latérales. L'Amérique du Nord. D'après les dessins origin aux pris sur les lieux par J. Milbert,* published by Henry Gaugain et Cie, Paris 1826
    Image 7 3/4 x 11 3/8 in.; sheet 13 x 15 in.
    Ref.: Stokes, vol. 3 (1918), pl. 569;
    Deák (1988), no. 299, no. 3
    Edwin Allen Cruikshank Collection, Gift of Susie Cruikshank Snyder, 1926
    The society owns five of Milbert's drawings and has a complete set of lithographs from the Itinéraire pittoresque du fleuve Hudson series, as well as a partial set.

11. CARL FREDRIK AKRELL (Swedish, 1779–1868) after BARON AXEL LEONHARD KLINCKOWSTRÖM (Swedish, 1775–1837)
View of Broadway, looking North from Ann Street, New York, as it appeared in 1819 1824

    Etching and aquatint, from *Atlas til Friherre Klinckowströms Bref om de Förenta Staterne,* published in Stockholm, 1824
    Image 8 x 15 in.; plate 11 3/4 x 18 1/2 in.; sheet 13 3/8 x 19 1/2 in.
    Ref.: Stokes, vol. 3 (1918), pl. 85, pp. 563–64;
    Deák (1988), no. 310
    Gift of the H. Dunscombe Colt Estate, 1982

12. WILLIAM JAMES BENNETT (American, born England, 1787–1844; to New York c. 1826)
Broadway from the Bowling Green

    Aquatint, from *Megarey's Street Views in the City of New-York,* c. 1834
    Image 9 7/8 x 13 3/8 in.; plate 11 5/8 x 15 3/8 inl.; page 14 x 20 3/4 in.
    Ref.: Stokes, vol. 3 (1918), pl. 98, pp. 589–90;
    Deák (1988), no. 350

Gift of Mrs. Ralph Smillie, 1969
Among the notable group of forty-six prints by Bennett in the New-York Historical Society's collection are all three prints he contributed to this Megarey series, bound with its original cover—the only installment the publisher managed to issue of the planned series. In addition, the society has a proof before letters.

13. WILLIAM JAMES BENNETT (American, born England, 1787–1844; to New York c. 1826)
South Street from Maiden Lane

    Aquatint, from *Megarey's Street Views in the City of New-York,* c. 1834
    Image 9 1/2 x 13 9/16 in.; plate 11 5/8 x 15 3/8 in.; page 14 x 20 3/4
    Ref.: Stokes, vol. 3 (1918), pl. 104–a, pp. 605–06;
    Deák (1988), no. 360
    Gift of Mrs. Ralph Smillie, 1969
    The society also has a proof of this print before letters (and before the addition of the iron pot and stick in the left foreground).

14. ALEXANDER JACKSON DAVIS (1803–1892)
Merchants' Exchange, New York 1827

    Lithograph on chine collé, from *Views of the Public Buildings in the City of New-York,* printed and published by Anthony Imbert, 79 Murray Street, New York
    Image 11 7/8 x 10 in.; chine 12 5/8 x 10 1/8 in.; sheet 18 7/8 x 15 in.
    Ref.: Stokes, vol. 3 (1918), pl. 102–b, p. 603
    Edwin Allen Cruikshank Collection, Gift of Susie Cruikshank Snyder, 1926
    The society possesses approximately 800 architectural drawings by Davis, including his designs for country villas and cottages, churches, and public buildings. A. J. Davis's original ink and wash rendering of this Merchants' Exchange elevation is held in the Edward W. C. Arnold Collection of New York Prints, Maps, and Pictures in the Metropolitan Museum of Art.

15. EDWARD WILLIAMS CLAY (1792–1857)
The Ruins of Phelp's & Peck's Store, Fulton Sreet, New York, as they appeared on the morning after the Accident of 4th May 1832

    Lithograph, published by John B. Pendleton 1832
    Image 9 1/4 x 12 in.; sheet 11 1/8 x 14 3/4 in.
    Ref.: Deák (1988), no. 401
    Gift of Beekman Family Association, through Dr. Fenwick Beekman, 1943

16. WILLIAM JAMES BENNETT (American, born England, 1787–1844; to New York c. 1826) after NICOLINO CALYO (American, born Italy, 1799–1884; to New York 1835)
View of the Great Fire in New York, December 16 & 17, 1835 as seen from the top of the Bank of America, corner of Wall and William Streets

    Hand-colored aquatint and etching, published by Lewis P. Clover, New York, 1836
    Image 16 3/8 x 23 5/8 in.; border 20 x 26 3/4 in.; sheet 21 1/4 x 27 3/4 in.
    Ref.: Stokes, vol. 3 (1918), pl. 114–a, p. 617;
    Deák (1988), no. 438
    Gift of the City of Detroit Historical Commission, 1955
    Nicolino Calyo's original gouache painting, on which this print is based, is also in the New-York Historical Society's collection, as is the original 25 by 30 inch copper plate used to make this print.

17. JOHN H. BUFFORD (1810–1870)
Ruins of the Merchants' Exchange after the Destructive Conflagration of December 16–17, 1835

    Hand-colored lithograph, printed by Nathaniel Currier; published by J. Disturnell, 156 Broadway, and J. H. Bufford, 19 Beekman Street, New York
    Image 9 x 12 1/4 in.; sheet 11 5/8 x 14 3/8 in.
    Gift of the H. Dunscombe Colt Estate, 1982

18. JOHN H. BUFFORD (1810–1870) after an architectural rendering by CYRUS L. WARNER (active in New York 1830–1850)
Merchants' Exchange, New York 1837
> Lithograph in brown and blue-gray tints with selected hand-coloring
> Image 15 1/4 x 22 in.; sheet 19 7/8 x 25 1/2 in.
> Ref.: Stokes, vol. 3 (1918), pl. 118, p. 623
> Herman N. Liberman, Jr. Collection, Gift of Hope Liberman Bach, 1977

19. UNKNOWN ARTIST
Burning of the American Theatre, Bowery, between Four & Five o'Clock on Thursday Morning, September 22, 1836
> Hand-colored lithograph, published by H. R. Robinson, New York, September 1836
> Image 8 3/4 x 12 in.; sheet 14 3/8 x 21 in.
> Purchase, 1939

20. WILLIAM JAMES BENNETT (American, born England, 1787–1844; to New York c. 1826) after JOHN WILLIAM HILL (American, born England, 1812–1879; to U.S. 1819)
New York from Brooklyn Heights 1837
> Hand-colored etching and aquatint, published by Lewis P. Clover, New York
> Image 19 3/4 x 31 3/4 in.; sheet (trimmed) 23 3/4 x 34 5/8 in.
> Ref.: Stokes, vol. 3 (1918), pl. 117, pp. 622–23; Deák (1988), no. 463
> Edwin Allen Cruikshank Collection, Gift of Susie Cruikshank Snyder, 1926
> *Only a few impressions of this print, which was a major achievement for its day, exist. The original copper plate is in the society's collection.*

WILLIAM JAMES BENNETT (American, born England, 1787–1844; to New York c. 1826) after FAYETTE B. TOWER (1817–1857)
> Four aquatints, from *Illustrations of the Croton Aqueduct*, published by Wiley & Putnam, New York, 1843
> Ref.: cf. Deák (1988), no. 526

21. *View above the Croton Dam, Plate IX*
> Image 5 1/2 x 10 1/2 in.; sheet 9 x 13 in.

22. *Croton Aqueduct at Mill River, Plate XV*
> Image 7 1/8 x 10 1/4 in.; sheet 9 1/4 x 13 in.

23. *Croton Aqueduct at Yonkers, Plate XVIII*
> Image 7 x 10 1/8 in.; sheet 9 1/4 x 13 in.

24. *View of the Jet at the Harlem River, Plate XX*
> Image 4 3/4 x 10 in.; sheet 9 1/2 x 13 in.
> Ref.: Stokes, vo. 3 (1918), pl A18–b, p. 875

25. NATHANIEL CURRIER (1813–1888)
The High Bridge at Harlem, New York 1849
> Lithograph, printed and published by Nathaniel Currier, 152 Nassau Street, New York
> Image 8 x 12 3/8 in.; sheet 13 1/2 x 17 7/8 in.
> Ref.: Gale, no. 3040
> Gift of Daniel Parish, Jr., 1899

26. CHARLES AUTENRIETH (active 1850) after Augustus Fay (c. 1824–?; active 1840s–1860)
Croton Water Reservoir from *Views of New York* 1850
> Color lithograph with selected hand-coloring, printed and published by Henry Hoff
> Image 6 1/8 x 8 7/8 in.; sheet/mount 11 x 13 3/4 in.
> Ref.: cf. Deák (1988), no. 597
> Purchase, 1922
> *Augustus Fay's original gouache drawing, on which this print is based, is in the collection of the New York Public Library.*

27. JOHN PENNIMAN (1817–1850)
Novelty Iron Works, Stillman, Allen & Co. Steam Engine and General Machinery Manufacturers, foot of 12th Street, East River, New York c. 1841–44
> Hand-colored lithograph, printed by George Endicott
> Image (within border) 19 x 31 1/2 in.; sheet 24 1/2 x 36 1/4 in.
> Purchase, Wilbur Fund, 1947

28. ROBERT HAVELL, JR. (English, 1793–1878; to U.S. 1839)
Panoramic View of New York, Taken from the North [Hudson] River 1844
> Hand-colored etching and aquatint, fifth state, printed by W. Neale; colored by Henry A. Havell and Thomas P. Spearing; published by Robert Havell, Sing Sing, New York, by William A. Colman, New York, and by Ackerman & Co., London
> Image 8 7/8 x 32 in.; plate 12 x 35 1/4 in.; sheet 13 x 37 in.
> Ref.: Stokes, vol. 3 (1918), pl. 123–a, pp. 685–86
> Gift of Daniel Parish, Jr., 1889

29. HENRY A. PAPPRILL (English, 1817–1896; active in New York c. 1846–1850) after FREDERICK CATHERWOOD (English, 1799–1854)
New-York Taken from the North West Angle of Fort Columbus, Governors Island [as it appeared in 1844] 1846
> Aquatint, published by Henry J. Megarey, New York
> Image 16 1/2 x 26 3/4 in.; plate 20 3/4 x 30 in.; sheet 26 3/16 x 40 in.
> Ref.: Stokes, vol. 3 (1918), pl. 131, pp. 697–98; Deák (1988), no. 531
> Gift of Victor W. von Hagen, 1949

30. G. MOORE

The New York Society Library—Frederick Diaper Architect c. 1840

Lithograph with tint stone, printed by [William] Day & [Louis] Haghe, London

Image 8 3/8 x 13 1/2 in.; sheet 12 1/4 x 18 1/4 in.

Gift of John B. Moreau, 1883

William Day (1797–1845) and Louis Haghe (1806–1895) were appointed "Lithographers to the Queen" in 1838.

31. GEORGE ENDICOTT (1802–1848) and WILLIAM ENDICOTT (1818–1850)

North Interior View of the New York Post Office as it Appeared on Feb. 1, 1845

Lithograph, printed by G. & W. Endicott, 22 John Street, New York 1845

Image 12 7/8 x 17 5/8 in.; sheet 19 x 29 in.

Ref.: Stokes, vol. 3 (1918), pl. 130–b, pp. 695–97; cf. Deák (1988), no. 530

Gift of Charles H. Brunie, 1953

The entire three-print set depicting the New York Post Office (exterior view, north interior view, and south interior view) are also in the society's collection, a 1845 gift from Postmaster John Lorimer Graham.

32. NATHANIEL CURRIER (1813–1888)

View of the Great Conflagration at New York, July 19th 1845, from the Corner of Broad and Stone Streets

Hand-colored lithograph, printed and published by Nathaniel Currier, 2 Spruce Street, New York, 1845

Image 8 1/8 x 12 3/8 in.; sheet 11 1/8 x 14 3/8 in.

Ref.: Gale, no. 6927

Gift of Eugene A. Hoffman, 1943

33. HENRY R. ROBINSON (active in New York (1843–1851), lithographer

Kipp and Brown's Stage as it Appeared in Passing the Astor House on the 16th Day of June 1845

Hand-colored lithograph, published by William H. Hoyt, 1845

Image 19 x 44 3/4 in.; sheet 23 1/2 x 47 1/2 in.

Gift of Robert G. Goelet, 1964

34. JAMES S. BAILLIE (active in New York 1838–1855)

The O'Connell Funeral Procession in the City of New York, September 22, 1847, with the Magnificent Cart drawn by Twelve Gray Horses richly caparisoned with black cloth trimmed with silver and bearing a shield with the Irish Harp

Hand-colored lithograph, printed and published by James Baillie, 87 St. near Third Avenue, New York

Image 7 7/8 x 12 1/2 in.; sheet 10 x 14 in.

Gift of Mrs. Geoffrey Hellman, 1979

35. JOHN BACHMANN (American, born Germany; active in New York 1849–1885)

New York City Hall, Park and Environs c. 1849

Lithograph, published by Williams & Stevens, 353 Broadway, New York

Image 11 7/8 x 17 7/8 in.; sheet 15 1/2 x 21 3/4 in.

Ref.: Deák (1988), no. 596

Edwin Allen Cruikshank Collection, Gift of Susie Cruikshank Snyder, 1926

The society's John McComb Architectural Drawings Collection boasts approximately 150 original architectural elevations, plans, sections, and detail drawings for City Hall, in addition to other designs for churches, public buildings, lighthouses, and fortifications.

36. HENRY PAPPRILL (English, 1817–1896; active in New York c. 1846–1850) after JOHN WILLIAM HILL (American, born England, 1812–1879; to U.S. 1819)

New York from the Steeple of St. Paul's Chapel Looking East, South and West 1849

Color aquatint (in brown, gray, green, turquoise, steel blue), proof, published by Henry J. Megarey, New York

Image 21 1/4 x 36 1/4 in.; sheet 27 5/8 x 41 1/2 in.

Ref.: Stokes, vol. 3 (1918), pl. 132, p. 698; Deák (1988), no. 578

Gift of Daniel Parish, Jr., 1899

Papprill's copper plate—the second he made during his New York sojourn—is also in the society's collection.

37. BENJAMIN FRANKLIN BUTLER (died c. 1865; active in New York c. 1846–1851)

Great Riot at the Astor Place Opera House, New York, Showing the dense Multitude of spectators when the Military fired, Killing and wounding about 70 persons 1849

Lithograph, published by Robert H. Elton, 90 Nassau Street, New York

Image (within border) 8 x 13 in.; sheet 14 5/8 x 18 1/4 in.

Purchase, 1886

38. CHARLES CURRIER (1818–1887)

Awful Explosion of a Steam Boiler belonging to A. B. Taylor & Co. Machinists, No. 5 and 7 Hague Street, on Monday, February 4th at a quarter to 8 o'clock wounding and killing about 120 persons 1850

Hand-colored lithograph, printed by C. Currier, 33 Spruce Street, New York

Image 11 1/2 x 9 1/4 in.; sheet 20 1/2 x 13 1/4 in.

Gift of Daniel Parish, Jr., 1899

39. FRANCIS D'AVIGNON (French, 1813–after 1865; active in New York c. 1843–1859) after Albert Hoffmann

El General Paez en Los Estados Unidos: Entrada del General Paez en Nueva York, Agosto 2 de 1850

Lithograph with tint stone

Image 11 x 14 3/4 in.; sheet 18 1/2 x 23 in.

Gift of Daniel Parish, Jr., 1902

40. NATHANIEL CURRIER (1813–1888)
First Appearance of Jenny Lind in America at Castle Garden, September 11, 1850
 Hand-colored lithograph, printed and published by
 Nathaniel Currier, 152 Nassau Street, corner of Spruce,
 Image 9 x 14 1/4 in.; sheet 12 3/8 x 19 in.
 Ref.: Gale, no. 2124
 Gift of George A. Zabriskie, 1946

41. EDWARD VALOIS (active 1840–1860) after JOHN BORNET
(active in New York c. 1852–1856)
Bay of New York, Taken from the Battery 1851
 Hand-colored lithograph, printed by David McLellan,
 26 Spruce Street, New York
 Image 13 1/2 x 36 1/2 in.; sheet 20 x 41 1/2 in.
 Ref.: Stokes, vol. 3 (1918), pl. 137–a, p. 705
 Purchase, 1963

42. FRANCES [FANNY] FLORA BOND PALMER (English,
1812–1875; to U.S. 1840s), for Currier & Ives
View on the Harlem River, New York with the High Bridge in the Distance 1852
 Hand-colored lithograph, printed and published by
 Currier & Ives
 Image 14 1/2 x 20 in.; sheet 18 1/2 x 20 1/2 in.
 Ref.: Stokes, vol. 3 (1918), p. 137–b, pp. 705–06; Gale, no.
 6958
 Bequest of Robert Goelet, 1966

43. AFTER CHARLES PARSONS (American, born England,
1821–1910; to U.S. 1830)
The Old Brewery at the Five Points, New York, as it Appeared on December 1, 1852, Previous to its Being Torn Down by the Ladies Home Missionary Society of the Methodist Episcopal Church
 Lithograph with tint stone, printed and published by
 Endicott & Co., New York
 Image 8 3/4 x 12 3/4 in.; sheet 11 3/4 x 15 1/4
 Gift of Mrs. John Kean, 1976

44. JOHN W. ORR (1815–1887) after CHARLES PARSONS
(American, born England, 1821–1910; U.S. 1830)
The Old Brewery at the Five Points, New York, as it Appeared by Candlelight, December 1852, When it Was Visited by About 20,000 People
 Wood engraving, printed by Oliver & Brother
 Image 6 x 9 in.; sheet 9 1/4 x 12 1/4 in.

45. FRANCIS MICHELIN and J. L. SHATTUCK [Michelin &
Shattuck, active as a partnership in New York, 1853–1854]
Home for the Friendless, New York City, under the Management of the American Female Guardian Society c. 1853–54
 Hand-colored lithograph
 Image 15 1/2 x 21 5/8 in.; sheet 20 x 24 in.
 Purchase, 1983

46. FRANÇOIS COURTIN (French, 1820–1871)
New-York Crystal Palace for the Exhibition of the Industry of All Nations 1853–54
 Hand-colored lithograph, printed and published by Turgis,
 Paris and New York
 Image 12 1/2 x 17 5/8 in.; sheet 19 1/8 x 23 2/4 in.
 Gift of Miss Adelaide Milton de Groot, 1941

47. WILLIAM NAUGLE (born 1817; active in New York
until after 1880)
Latting Observatory near Sixth Avenue between 42nd and 43rd Streets, New York, Built as Part of the Exhibition of the Industry of All Nations 1853
 Lithograph with tint stone, printed by [Alexander] Robertson
 & [Henry] Seibert Lithography,
 121 Fulton Street, New York
 Image (within border) 19 1/4 x 14 5/8 in.;
 sheet 24 x 18 1/2 in
 Ref.: Deák (1988), no., 658
 Purchase, 1928

48. CHARLES PARSONS (American, born England, 1821–1910;
to U.S. 1830)
An Interior View of the Crystal Palace 1853
 Lithograph with tint stone, printed by Endicott & Co.;
 published by George S. Appleton, New York
 Image 13 1/2 x 20 3/8 in.; sheet 16 3/8 x 23 in.
 Gift of Daniel Parish, Jr., 1904

49. UNKNOWN ARTIST
The Destruction by Fire of the New York Crystal Palace, Oct. 5, 1858
 Hand-colored lithograph, published by H. H. Lloyd & Co.,
 and by Spearing & Stutzman, Appleton's Building, New York
 Image 20 3/8 x 31 in.; sheet 24 x 33 1/2 in.
 Purchase, Wilbur Fund, 1943

50. JOHN BORNET (active in New York c. 1852–1856)
Panorama of the Harbor of New York, Staten Island, and the Narrows 1854
 Lithograph with tan and blue-gray tint stone, printed by
 [Louis] Nagel & [Adam] Weingärtner, New York; published
 by Goupil & Co., New York
 Image (within border) 23 1/4 x 36 1/4 in.;
 sheet 29 3/8 x 37 7/8 in.
 Edwin Allen Cruikshank Collection, Gift of Susie
 Cruikshank Snyder, 1926

51. JOHN BORNET (active in New York c. 1852–1856)
Panorama of Manhattan Island, City of New York and Environs 1854
 Hand-colored lithograph with tint border, printed by Adam
 Weingärtner of Nagel & Weingärtner, New York;
 published by Goupil & Co., New York
 Image (with border) 25 1/4 x 38 1/4 in. (at highest point);
 sheet 28 3/8 x 40 in.
 Purchase, 1923

52. SIGISMOND HIMELY (French, 1801–1872) after JOHN WILLIAM HILL (American, born England, 1812–1879; to U.S. 1819)
New York 1855
    Aquatint, printed by McQueen, London; published by
    Francis and George Warren Smith, New York
    Image (margins trimmed) 29 x 50 3/4 in.
    Ref.: Stokes, vol. 3 (1918), p. 714; Deák (1988), no. 643;
    cf. Koke, no. 1218
    Gift of Mrs. John Galey, 1953
    John William Hill's watercolor is in the society's collection.

53. FREDERICK HEPPENHEIMER (German, 1826–1878; active in New York after 1850)
View of Liberty Street, New York, from Broadway to Greenwich Street c. 1855–56
    Hand-colored lithograph
    Image (within border) 19 x 34 3/4 in.; sheet 23 3/8 x 36 3/4 in.

54. JOHN LAWRENCE GILES (active in New York 1876–1882), artist and lithographer
Scene in the New Russian Baths, No. 18 La Fayette Place c. 1876–78
    Lithograph, printed by Charles Hart
    Image 11 1/4 x 17 3/4 in.; sheet 14 x 19 5/8 in.
    Purchase, Wilbur Fund, 1942

55. THOMAS BENECKE (active in New York 1855–1856)
Sleighing in New York 1855
    Color lithograph with hand-coloring, printed by
    Nagel & Lewis, 122 Fulton Street, New York;
    published by Emil Seitz, 413 Broadway, New York
    Image 21 1/4 x 30 1/2 in. (sheet trimmed to image)
    Ref.: Deák (1976), p. 107
    Edwin Allen Cruikshank Collection, Gift of Susie
    Cruikshank Snyder, 1926

56. JOHN BACHMANN (American, born Germany; active in New York 1849–1885), artist, lithographer, and publisher
New York & Environs 1861
    Lithograph and tan tint stone, printed by Conrad Fatzer
    Image 20 1/4 in. diameter; sheet (trimmed to octagonal
    shape) 22 7/8 x 22 3/4 in. (at tallest and widest points)
    Edwin Allen Cruikshank Collection, Gift of Susie
    Cruikshank Snyder, 1926

57. JOSEPH C. GEISSLER (active in New York 1860–1865) after PIERRE (?) MARTEL
Martel's New York Central Park, Respectfully Dedicated to the Park Commissioners 1864
    Lithograph with pink and gray-blue tint stones, printed by
    Henry C. Eno; published by William H. Shields, New York
    Image 23 1/4 x 36 1/4 in.; sheet 30 x 40 3/4 in.
    Ref.: Stokes, vol. 3 (1918), pl. 151, p. 771;
    Deák (1988), no. 790
    Purchase, 1952

58. After THURE DE THULSTRUP (Swedish, 1848–1930; to U.S. via Canada c. 1875)
Sleighing in Central Park, New York City
    Wood engraving, from *Harper's Weekly*, February 18, 1888
    Image 13 5/8 x 19 3/4 in.; sheet 16 x 22 1/4 in.
    Gift of Harry T. Peters, 1946

59. SARONY, MAJOR & KNAPP, lithographers [NAPOLEON SARONY (born Quebec 1821–1896; to New York c. 1836); in partnership with Richard Major and Joseph F. Knapp, 1857–c. 1864]
Archway under Carriage Drive for Traffic Road across Central Park c. 1860–64
    Lithograph with tint stone
    Image 6 1/8 x 9 1/4 in.; sheet 10 x 12 1/4 in.
    Purchase, Wilbur Fund, 1945

60. LYMAN W. ATWATER (1835–1891) after CHARLES PARSONS (American, born England, 1821–1910; to U.S. 1830)
Central-Park, Winter: The Skating Pond 1862
    Hand-colored lithograph, printed and published by
    Currier & Ives
    Image: 18 x 26 3/4 in.; sheet 25 x 33 1/8 in.
    Ref.: Gale, no. 1047

61. ENDICOTT & Co., lithographer
Harlem Bridge Now Being Erected across the Harlem River at the Terminus of the Third Avenue, New York 1864
    Lithograph printed in gray, tan, and pale blue-green tints
    Image (within border) 13 1/4 x 32 1/4 in.;
    sheet 19 3/4 x 35 1/4 in
    Gift of Daniel Parish, Jr., 1901

62. UNKNOWN ARTIST
Presentation of Colors to the 20th U.S. Colored Infantry, Colonel N. B. Bartram, at the Union League Club House, New York, March 5, 1864
    Wood engraving, from *Frank Leslie's Illustrated Newspaper*,
    March 26, 1864
    Image 12 1/2 x 17 5/8 in.
    Gift of Daniel Parish, Jr., 1904

63. ENDICOTT & Co., lithographer
Continental Works, Green Point, Brooklyn, T. F. Rowland, Proprietor c. 1865
    Hand-colored lithograph
    Image (within border) 18 1/4 x 33 1/4 in.;
    sheet 26 x 38 3/4 in.
    Gift of Natalie W. Peters, Harry T. Peters, Jr., and Natalie P.
    Webster, 1962

64. After a photograph by Rockwood & Co., New York
Submarine Mining Operations at Hallet's Point 1871
    Wood engraving, from *Harper's Weekly*, September 23, 1871
    Image 13 7/8 x 9 1/2 in.; sheet 16 1/4 x 11 in.

65. CHARLES R. PARSONS (1844–1920) and LYMAN W. ATWATER (1835–1891)
The Port of New York: Bird's Eye View from the Battery, Looking South 1878
Color lithograph, published by Currier & Ives
Image 20 3/4 x 33 1/16 in.; sheet 25 1/2 x 37 in.
Ref.: Gale, no. 5258
Purchase, 1923
The society has an 1872 color lithograph version of this same view, which is almost identical but shows slightly fewer ships (the earlier harbor view lacking the most modern models depicted in the 1878 print) and slightly fewer pedestrians.

66. F. LEO HUNTER (1862–1943)
Coenties Slip, South Street 1881
Etching
Plate 12 3/8 x 18 5/8 in.; sheet 16 3/8 x 22 1/8 in.
Gift of James Boyd, presented in memory of his wife Agnes Gray Boyd, 1935

67. UNKNOWN ARTIST
New York Tower (W. A. Roebling, Engineer) [under Construction for the East River Bridge] September 1872
Lithograph
Image 9 3/4 x 12 7/8 in.; sheet 12 x 15 7/8 in.

68. UNKNOWN ARTIST
Bird's Eye View of the Great New York and Brooklyn Bridge and Grand Display of Fireworks on Opening Night 1883
Color lithograph in black, green, and red, published by A. Major
Image 15 1/4 x 24 1/4 in.; sheet 18 x 25 3/4 in.
Purchase, 1940

69. HORACE BAKER (1833–1918) after a watercolor by F. HOPKINSON SMITH (1838–1915)
Under the Towers
Wood engraving, from *Harper's Weekly*, February 18, 1882
Image 13 1/2 x 8 1/2 in.; sheet 16 1/2 x 11 1/2 in.

70. CURRIER & IVES (NATHANIEL CURRIER [1813–1895] and JAMES MERRITT IVES [1824–1895]; partnership formed 1857), lithographer and publisher
The Great East River Suspension Bridge Connecting the Cities of New York & Brooklyn, Showing Also the Splendid Panorama of the Bay and the Port of New York, 1885
Color lithograph
Image 21 x 34 1/8 in.; sheet 25 3/4 x 36 in.
Ref.: Gale, no. 2683
Purchase, 1964

71. CURRIER & IVES (NATHANIEL CURRIER [1813–1895] and JAMES MERRITT IVES [1824–1895]; partnership formed 1857), lithographer and publisher
The Great Bartholdi Statue, Liberty Enlightening the World—The Gift of France to the American People to be Erected on Bedloe's Island, New York Harbor 1883
Color lithograph
Image 25 5/8 x 21 1/4 in.; sheet 31 1/16 x 25 1/4 in.
Ref.: Gale, no. 2788

72. CURRIER & IVES (NATHANIEL CURRIER [1813–1895] and JAMES MERRITT IVES [1824–1895]; partnership formed 1857), lithographer and publisher
The Great Bartholdi Statue, Liberty Enlightening the World—The Gift of France to the American People, Erected on Bedloe's Island, New York Harbor, and Unveiled October, 28th, 1886
Color lithograph, copyrighted 1885; published 1886
Image 24 1/16 x 16 7/7 in.; sheet 31 x 20 7/8 in.
Ref.: Gale, no. 2792
Gift of Samuel V. Hoffman, 1927

73. AMERICAN PHOTO-LITHOGRAPHY CO., New York
Broadway, North from Cortlandt and Maiden Lane c. 1885–87
Color photo-lithograph, published by James J. Fogerty, New York
Image 25 1/2 x 31 1/2 in.; sheet 28 x 34 in.

74. CHARLES F. W. MIELATZ (American, born Germany, 1864–1919; to U.S. 1867)
Entrance to Brooklyn Bridge 1892
Etching on Japanese paper
Plate 12 7/8 x 8 3/4 in.; sheet 15 x 11 in.

75. CHARLES F. W. MIELATZ (American, born Germany, 1864–1919; to U.S. 1867)
Cherry Street 1904
Etching
Image 11 7/8 x 7 3/8 in.; sheet 17 1/2 x 10 3/4 in.

76. CHARLES F. W. MIELATZ (American, born Germany, 1864–1919; to U.S. 1867)
The Tombs 1889
Etching, later state
Plate 11 x 8 in.; sheet 13 1/2 x 10 1/2 in.
Gift of James Boyd, presented in memory of his wife Agnes Gray Boyd, 1935

77. EDWIN DAVIS FRENCH (1851–1906)
The Murray Hill Distributing Reservoir 1897
Engraving, published by the New York Society of Iconophiles (Series 1, No. 11, January 1897)
Image 3 x 4 in.; plate 4 1/2 x 5 3/8 in.; sheet 8 x 10 in.
Gift of Mrs. John Adams Dix, 1958
The New-York Historical Society has almost a complete set of prints issued by the Society of Iconophiles. In addition, its book plate collection includes numerous examples of French's work.

78. CHARLES F. W. MIELATZ (American, born Germany, 1864–1919; to U.S. 1867)
The Lych Gate (Little Church around the Corner) 1902–06
Etching in brown ink on Japanese paper
Plate 10 3/4 x 7 7/8 in.; sheet 13 3/8 x 10 in.

79. CHARLES F. W. MIELATZ (American, born Germany, 1864–1919; to U.S. 1867)
Restaurant in Mott Street 1906
Etching
Plate 9 7/8 x 6 1/4 in.; sheet 12 3/4 x 8 1/2 in.

80. CHARLES F. W. MIELATZ (American, born Germany, 1864–1919; to U.S. 1867)
Balcony in Pell Street 1908
Four-color etching, second state, on Japanese paper
Plate 10 x 7 in.; sheet 13 x 9 7/8 in.
Gift of James Boyd, presented in memory of his wife Agnes Gray Boyd, 1935

81. JOSEPH PENNELL (1857–1926)
Rebuilding Fifth Avenue 1908
Etching
Plate 11 1/8 x 8 1/2 in.; sheet 13 x 8 1/2 in.
Ref.: Wuerth, no. 493

82. JOSEPH PENNELL (1857–1926)
St. Paul's, New York 1915
Etching
Plate 10 7/8 x 8 1/2 in.; sheet 13 1/4 x 9 in.
Ref.: Wuerth, no. 678
Gift of James Boyd, presented in memory of his wife Agnes Gray Boyd, 1935

83. HENRI DEVILLE (French, 1871–?; active in U.S. 1902–1914)
City Hall Park 1911
Etching
Plate 7 1/8 x 4 1/2 in.; sheet 8 x 5 in.

84. JOHN SLOAN (1871–1951)
Washington Arch 1923
Etching
Plate 7 7/8 x 4 3/4 in.; sheet 12 3/8 x 9 1/2 in.
Ref.: Morse, no. 212
Gift of James Boyd, presented in memory of his wife Agnes Gray Boyd, 1935

85. JOHN SLOAN (1871–1951)
Easter Eve, Washington Square 1926
Etching and aquatint (on zinc)
Plate 9 7/8 x 7 3/4 in.; sheet 12 3/4 x 10 5/8 in.
Ref.: Morse, no. 222
Gift of James Boyd, presented in memory of his wife Agnes Gray Boyd, 1935

86. FREDERICK K. DETWILLER (1882–1953)
Williamsburg Bridge July 4, 1924
Etching and aquatint
Plate 17 1/4 x 10 7/8 in.; sheet 20 3/4 x 15 1/4 in.
Gift of James Boyd, presented in memory of his wife Agnes Gray Boyd, 1944

87. ADOLF TREIDLER (1886–1981)
Help Complete New York's Great Cathedral, A Shrine of Worship for All People 1925
Color lithograph poster, published by Carey & Sons
Image 20 1/2 x 12 5/8 in.; sheet 20 1/4 x 14 1/8 in.
Gift of the Committee for completing the Cathedral of St. John the Divine, through Dr. William S. Thomas, 1925

88. FREDERICK K. DETWILLER (1882–1953)
Building the Nave, Cathedral of St. John the Divine, New York City June 1925
Etching and aquatint
Plate 11 7/8 x 16 7/8 in.; sheet 15 1/4 x 20 1/2 in.
Gift of James Boyd, presented in memory of his wife Agnes Gray Boyd, 1935

89. WILLIAM C. MCNULTY (1889–1963)
Building with Steel, Paramount Building on Broadway between 43rd to 44th Streets 1926
Drypoint
Plate 12 7/8 x 10 1/4 in.; sheet 18 1/2 x 12 1/2 in.
Gift of James Boyd, presented in memory of his wife Agnes Gray Boyd, 1935
The society has thirty-seven New York City prints by William C. McNulty in its collection. Although this group demonstrates that he was a highly skilled printmaker of New York's architecture and street scenes, few publications exist to document his graphic work and career.

90. WILLIAM C. MCNULTY (1889–1963)
Demolishing Old Madison Square Garden, Fourth Avenue and 26th Street 1927
Drypoint and etching, trial proof
Plate 8 1/8 x 10 3/8 in.; sheet 11 1/2 x 15 1/8 in.
Gift of James Boyd, presented in memory of his wife Agnes Gray Boyd, 1935
The New-York Historical Society has both an early trial proof of McNulty's print (without the sky filled in, making the contrast of the cranes more striking against the old building), as well as a final editioned impression. Of related interest is the society's McKim, Mead & White Architectural Drawings Collection, containing more than 48,000 items.

91. WILLIAM C. MCNULTY (1889–1963)
Demolishing the Century Theatre, Central Park West and 63rd Street 1930
Drypoint
Plate 8 5/8 x 11 1/8 in.; sheet 13 3/4 x 17 1/4 in.
Gift of James Boyd, presented in memory of his wife Agnes Gray Boyd, 1935

92. ANTON SCHUTZ (American, born Germany, 1894–1977; to U.S. 1924)
Metropolis from Governors Island c. 1927
Etching
Plate 10 x 13 3/4 in.; sheet 14 x 19 in.
The New-York Historical Society has 123 prints by Anton Schutz. Representing the largest group of prints by a single twentieth-century artist, the Schutz holdings constitute (at this writing) the most extensive representation of the artist's work in any of the major New York graphic art repositories. In 1940, Schutz stopped etching; he cancelled most of his copper plates and donated them to the war effort as scrap metal. After World War II, he more actively led his business, the New York Graphic Society.

93. ANTON SCHUTZ (American, born Germany, 1894–1977;
to U.S. 1924)
Gateway to Wall Street at Broadway 1930
Etching
Plate 13 7/8 x 9 3/4 in.; sheet 19 x 13 3/4 in.
Gift of James Boyd, presented in memory of his wife Agnes
Gray Boyd, 1935

94. TAVIK FRANTIŠEK ŠIMON (Bohemian, 1877–1942)
New York Stock Exchange 1927
Color soft-ground etching and aquatint
Plate 17 1/4 x 13 3/8 in.; sheet 24 x 18 3/4 in.
Ref.: Campbell, no. 251
Purchase, Wilbur Fund, 1956
*The New-York Historical Society's George B. Post Architectural
Record Collection houses over 8,600 architectural drawings
and blueprints (c. 1860–1950), including some designs for this
building, along with other important archival documentation.*

95. JOSEPH W. GOLINKEN (1896–1977)
Interior of the Stock Exchange
Lithograph
Image 20 5/8 x 15 1/2 in.; sheet 23 1/2 x 18 1/4 in.
Herman N. Liberman, Jr. Collection, Gift of Hope Liberman
Bach, 1977
*This is one of three Golinken prints in the society's collection.
Most of Golinken's lithographs were made in the late 1920s and
1930s. He was known primarily as a leading sports artist, who
also distinguished himself in a naval career in both world wars,
including his distinguished service as an Admiral during World
War II.*

96. CHILDE HASSAM (1859–1935)
Floor of the Stock Exchange, January 7, 8, and 9, 1927
Etching
Plate 9 5/8 x 14 5/8 in.; sheet 13 1/2 x 18 1/4 in.
Ref.: Cortissoz & Clayton, no. 266
Gift of Kiliaen Van Rensselaer, 1945

97. TAVIK FRANTIŠEK ŠIMON (Bohemian, 1877–1942)
New York-Brooklyn Bridge 1927
Color soft ground etching and aquatint
Plate 14 x 16 3/8 in.; sheet 19 3/8 x 23 3/4 in.
Ref.: Campbell, no. 248
Purchase, Wilbur Fund, 1956

98. WILLIAM C. MCNULTY (1889–1963)
Woolworth Building, New York 1929
Drypoint
Plate 13 1/8 x 9 in.; sheet 17 1/4 x 11 5/8 in.
Gift of James Boyd, presented in memory of his wife Agnes
Gray Boyd, 1935

99. HIROSHI YOSHIDA (Japanese, 1876–1950)
New York, Woolworth Building 1928
Color woodcut
Image 5 x 3 1/4 in.; sheet 10 1/8 x 7 1/4 in.
Ref.: Ogura, no. 111
Gift of James Boyd, presented in memory of his wife Agnes
Gray Boyd, 1935

100. SAMUEL CHAMBERLAIN (1895–1975)
The Curving Canyon, New York 1929
Drypoint on paper verdâtre
Plate 8 3/4 x 5 3/4 in.; sheet 11 3/4 x 7 1/2 in.
Gift of James Boyd, presented in memory of his wife Agnes
Gray Boyd, 1935

101. WILLIAM C. MCNULTY (1889–1963)
Roaring Forties, New York 1929
Etching with drypoint
Plate 12 1/4 x 8 7/8 in.; sheet 17 1/4 x 11 5/8 in.
Gift of James Boyd, presented in memory of his wife Agnes
Gray Boyd, 1935

102. ANTON SCHUTZ (American, born Germany, 1894–1977;
to U.S. 1924)
*The Great White Way Looking toward Times Square
from 49th Street* 1931
Etching and aquatint
Plate 14 x 10 in.; sheet 18 3/8 x 11 3/4 in.
Gift of James Boyd, presented in memory of his wife Agnes
Gray Boyd, 1935

103. ANTON SCHUTZ (American, born Germany, 1894–1977;
to U.S. 1924)
*Lower Manhattan Seen from 2 Montague Terrace,
Brooklyn Heights* 1931
Color aquatint on yellow tinted paper
Plate 9 7/8 x 13 7/8 in.; sheet 13 5/8 x 17 1/2 in.
Gift of James Boyd, presented in memory of his wife Agnes
Gray Boyd, 1935

104. ANTON SCHUTZ (American, born Germany, 1894–1977;
to U.S. 1924)
*Plaza Lights, Looking Downtown from Central Park
and 65th Street* 1931
Aquatint on turquoise paper
Plate 9 7/8 x 13 7/8 in.; sheet 13 5/8 x 18 1/4 in.
Gift of James Boyd, presented in memory of his wife Agnes
Gray Boyd, 1935

105. WILLIAM C. MCNULTY (1889–1963)
Docks, Fulton Market
Drypoint
Plate 12 x 8 7/8 in.; sheet 18 5/8 x 13 7/8 in.
Gift of James Boyd, presented in memory of his wife Agnes
Gray Boyd, 1935

106. WILLIAM C. MCNULTY (1889–1963)
Under Brooklyn Bridge 1931
Drypoint
Plate 9 3/8 x 12 7/8 in.; sheet 14 1/8 x 18 1/4 in.
Gift of James Boyd, presented in memory of his wife Agnes
Gray Boyd, 1935

107. ERNEST FIENE (1894–1965)
New York Skyline 1932
    Lithograph, printed by George C. Miller
    Image 12 3/4 x 17 1/2 in.; sheet 16 x 22 7/8 in.
    Purchase, 1983

108. ERNEST D. ROTH (American, born Germany, 1879–1964;
to U.S. 1882)
*Financial Towers, Downtown New York between Wall
Street and Old Slip* 1935
    Etching
    Plate 12 x 15 in.; sheet 14 5/8 x 17 1/2 in.
    Gift of James Boyd, presented in memory of his wife Agnes
    Gray Boyd, 1936

109. FREDERICK K. DETWILLER (1882–1953)
*Pylons, Hudson Bridge, View Between 176–177
Streets, New York City* November 17, 1928
    Etching and aquatint with hand coloring
    Plate 16 3/4 x 11 5/8 in.; sheet 20 1/2 x 15 1/4 in.
    Gift of James Boyd, presented in memory of his wife Agnes
    Gray Boyd, 1944
    *In addition to Cass Gilbert's extraordinary architectural draw
    ings for the Hudson (or George Washington) Bridge, the society
    possesses Ernest Lyman Scott's George Washington Bridge
    Construction Photograph Collection (1929–31).*

110. GOTTLOB L. BRIEM (American, born Germany,
1899–1972; to U.S. 1926)
Power, Washington Bridge, New York City 1931
    Etching
    Plate 14 3/4 x 9 1/2 in.; 19 7/8 x 12 3/4 in.
    Gift of James Boyd, presented in memory of his wife Agnes
    Gray Boyd, 1935
    *The society possesses ten of Briem's original plates, including
    those for this print and for cat. no. 111, as well as proof
    impressions.*

111. GOTTLOB L. BRIEM (American, born Germany,
1899–1972; to U.S. 1926)
Tower under Construction, Washington Bridge 1931
    Etching
    Plate 14 3/4 x 9 1/2 in.; 19 7/8 x 12 3/4 in.
    Gift of James Boyd, presented in memory of his wife Agnes
    Gray Boyd, 1935

112. ANTON SCHUTZ (American, born Germany, 1894–1977;
to U.S. 1924)
*George Washington Bridge Showing Manhattan
Approaches* 1932
    Etching, second state
    Image 9 7/8 x 13 7/8 in.; sheet 11 1/2 x 18 1/4 in.
    Gift of James Boyd, presented in memory of his wife Agnes
    Gray Boyd, 1935

113. ALBERT FLANAGAN (1886–1969)
Towers of Manhattan, 42nd Street Group 1930
    Etching
    Plate 12 3/4 x 6 3/8 in.; sheet 17 x 10 1/4 in.
    Gift of Mrs. Albert E. Flanagan, 1969
    *This print is a fitting complement to the construction progress
    photographs found in the society's Irving Browning Photograph
    Collection (1920s–1930s).*

114. WALTER TITTLE (1883–1966)
Manhattan Minarets 1931
    Drypoint
    Plate 14 5/8 x 9 in.; sheet 17 7/8 x 11 1/4 in.
    Purchase, 1937

115. WERNER DREWES (American, born Germany, 1899–1985;
to U.S. 1930)
Empire State Building 1931
    Drypoint and roulette
    Plate 12 3/4 x 4 1/4 in.; sheet 17 3/4 x 8 7/8 in.
    Ref.: Rose, no. 167
    Gift of James Boyd, presented in memory of his wife Agnes
    Gray Boyd, 1935

116. ANTON SCHUTZ (German, 1894–1977; to U.S. 1924)
*The Empire State Building Seen from 29th Street and
the Hotel Seville* [also called *The Old and the New*]
1932
    Etching, second state of first proof
    Plate 14 x 10 in.; 17 3/4 x 11 7/8 in.
    Gift of James Boyd, presented in memory of his wife Agnes
    Gray Boyd, 1935

117. CHESTER B. PRICE (1885–1962)
Manhattan Forum c. 1931–32
    Drypoint
    Plate 10 1/4 x 7 7/8 in.; sheet 14 1/8 x 9 7/8 in.
    Purchase, 1937

118. WILLIAM MEYEROWITZ (American, born Russia,
1887–1981; to U.S. 1908)
Modern New York 1933
    Etching
    Plate 11 7/8 x 10 in.; sheet 13 5/8 x 11 1/8 in.
    Purchase, 1983

119. MORTIMER BORNE (American, born Poland, 1902–1987;
to U.S. 1916)
*Central Synagogue [formerly Congregation Ahawath
Chesed], Lexington Avenue at 55th Street* 1931
    Drypoint
    Plate 7 7/8 x 5 7/8 in.; sheet 11 1/2 x 9 1/8 in.
    Gift of Noel J. Blackman, 1979

120. MORTIMER BORNE (American, born Poland, 1902–1987;
to U.S. 1916)
Temple Emanu-El from Central Park 1931
    Drypoint
    Plate 9 7/8 x 6 7/8 in.; sheet 14 1/4 x 10 5/8 in.
    Gift of Noel J. Blackman, 1979

121. JAMES PENNEY (1910–1982)

Subway 1932

Lithograph

Image 12 1/4 x 17 1/4 in.; sheet 15 3/8 x 20 3/8 in.

Purchase, 1982

The New-York Historical Society has approximately 50,000 photographs documenting the New York City subway construction from about 1900 to 1940.

122. MORTIMER BORNE (American, born Poland, 1902–1987; to U.S. 1916)

Hooverville (on Hudson) 1934

Drypoint

Plate 6 7/8 x 9 7/8 in.; sheet 10 x 12 7/8 in.

Gift of Noel J. Blackman, 1979

123. ERNEST D. ROTH (American, born Germany, 1879–1964; to U.S. 1882)

Queensboro Bridge, Manhattan, from Welfare Island 1935

Etching

Plate 9 5/8 x 15 in.; sheet 12 3/8 x 17 1/2 in.

Gift of James Boyd, presented in memory of his wife Agnes Gray Boyd, 1936

124. MABEL DWIGHT (1876–1955)

Old Greenwich Village 1928

Lithograph

Image 9 1/2 x 9 1/2 in.; sheet 16 x 11 1/2 in.

Ref.: Robinson and Pirog, no. 22

125. FRANK [FRANCIS JOSEPH] HANLEY (1913–?)

Jefferson Market Clock c. 1933–37 (?)

Linocut

Image 11 7/8 x 9 in.; sheet 13 7/8 x 11 in.

126. LOU BARLOW (born 1908)

Sweet Potato Man 1936

Wood engraving, stamped "New York City WPA Art Project"

Image 6 x 4 1/2 in.; sheet 11 3/8 x 8 3/4 in.

Purchase, 1983

127. WILLIAM C. MCNULTY (1889–1963)

The Orange Cart, Orchard Street, New York 1934

Etching

Plate 12 1/8 x 8 3/4 in.; sheet 15 3/4 x 10 7/8 in.

Gift of James Boyd, presented in memory of his wife Agnes Gray Boyd, 1935

128. BETTY WALDO PARISH (American, born Germany, 1910–1986; to U.S. c. 1926)

Marketing on Avenue A 1936

Etching

Plate 9 x 11 3/4 in.; sheet 11 1/2 x 16 1/8 in.

Gift of the artist in memory of her father, William F. Parish, 1955

129. ALBERT E. FLANAGAN (1886–1969)

The Fountain, Central Park, New York 1933

Drypoint

Plate 9 3/4 x 6 1/4 in.; sheet 16 1/4 x 10 1/2 in.

Gift of Mrs. Albert E. Flanagan, 1969

130. JULIUS F. GAYLER (1872–1948)

The Eternal Light, New York 1935

Etching and aquatint

Plate 10 1/2 x 6 1/4 in.; sheet 12 1/4 x 8 1/2 in.

Gift of the artist, 1941

131. EDITH NANKIVELL (1896–1984)

Eternal Light, Madison Square 1937

Etching and aquatint

Plate 10 x 5 1/16 in.; sheet 12 9/16 x 7 1/4 in.

Gift of James Boyd, presented in memory of his wife Agnes Gray Boyd, 1935

132. JULIUS F. GAYLER (1872–1948)

Saint Paul's Chapel, New York 1939

Etching and aquatint, first state

Plate 10 1/2 x 7 1/2 in.; sheet 12 5/8 x 9 in.

Gift of the artist, 1941

133. ERNEST D. ROTH (American, born Germany, 1879–1964; to U.S. 1882)

Library of Columbia University, New York City 1933

Etching

Plate 11 x 13 7/8 in.; sheet 13 3/8 x 16 3/8 in.

Gift of James Boyd, presented in memory of his wife Agnes Gray Boyd, 1936

The New-York Historical Society's extensive McKim, Mead & White collection includes architectural drawings for this library.

134. MARTIN LEWIS (American, born Australia, 1882–1962; to U.S. 1900)

Chance Meeting 1940–41

Drypoint, published by the Society of American Etchers

Plate 10 7/16 x 7 1/2 in.; sheet 15 1/2 x 10 3/4 in.

Ref.: McCarron, no. 131

Gift of Madeleine Grant, 2002

135. MORTIMER BORNE (American, born Poland, 1902–1987; to U.S. 1916)

Chinatown, Doyers Street 1940

Drypoint

Plate 7 x 10 in.; sheet 8 3/4 x 13 3/8 in.

Gift of Noel J. Blackman, 1979

Of the more than four hundred prints Mortimer Borne made after 1926, including a preponderance of New York City views, the society has eighty-one. This collection ranks second to that of the Metropolitan Museum of Art, which has one hundred Borne prints.

136. MORTIMER BORNE (American, born Poland, 1902–1987;
to U.S. 1916)
Henry Street, Brooklyn Heights 1941
Drypoint
Plate 9 7/8 x 7 in.; sheet 14 3/8 x 10 3/8 in.
Gift of Noel J. Blackman, 1979

137. RALPH FABRI (American, born Hungary, 1894–1975; to
U.S. 1921)
A Day in the Park c. 1942
Etching with drypoint
Plate 9 7/8 x 8 in.; sheet 13 x 10 1/8 in.
Purchase, 1986

138. BETTY WALDO PARISH (American, born Germany,
1910–1986; to U.S. c. 1926)
*East of Gramercy (22nd Street between Third and
Second Avenues)*, 1950–51
Wood engraving
Image 15 7/8 x 9 7/8 in.; sheet 17 1/2 x 11 1/4 in.
Gift of the artist in memory of her father, William F. Parish,
1955

139. BETTY WALDO PARISH (American, born Germany,
1910–1986; to U.S. c. 1926)
Encroachment of a City—Lower Battery Park
1946–52
Engraving
Plate 15 7/8 x 11 in.; sheet 18 1/4 x 13 5/8 in.
Gift of the artist in memory of her father, William F. Parish,
1955

140. RICHARD HAAS (born 1936)
Little Singer Building 1971
Etching
Plate 35 5/8 x 13 5/8 in.; sheet 41 1/2 x 18 3/8 in.
Gift of Harmon H. Goldstone, 1974

141. RICHARD HAAS (born 1936)
Flatiron Building 1973
Etching
Plate 35 3/8 x 12 7/8 in.; 41 1/2 x 18 3/8 in.
Gift of Harmon H. Goldstone, 1974

142. [ARTHUR] JOHN HARRIS (born 1959)
Flatiron 1993
Etching
Image: 33 1/4 x 23 3/4 in.; sheet 41 x 29 1/8 in.
Purchase, 1993

143. RICHARD SLOAT (born 1945)
Rising Sun 1977
Aquatint
Image 24 3/8 x 17 7/8 in.; sheet 31 x 22 1/4 in.
Gift of the artist, 2004

144. ALAN PETRULIS (born 1954)
White Street 1977
Etching
Plate 5 3/4 x 8 3/4 in.; sheet 8 1/4 x 12 1/2 in.
Gift of the artist, 2004

145. LAWRENCE NELSON WILBUR (1897–1988)
Old Brownstones, New York c. 1983
Drypoint
Plate 9 7/8 x 12 3/8 in.; sheet 15 3/4 x 18 1/8 in.

146. MAX FERGUSON (born 1959)
Subterraneans X. Spring Street 1985
Etching
Plate 17 x 24 3/4 in.; sheet 22 1/2 x 29 5/8 in.
Gift of the artist, 1985

147. WILLIAM BEHNKEN (born 1943)
Bronx Crossing 1991
Aquatint
Plate 18 x 24 in.; sheet 22 1/4 x 29 7/8 in.
Gift of the artist, 2004

148. CRAIG MCPHERSON (born 1948)
FDR Drive 1993
Mezzotint
Plate 35 1/2 x 23 3/4 in.; sheet 42 x 29 5/8 in.
Gift of the artist, 2004

149. ART WERGER (born 1955)
Early Thaw 1996
Mezzotint
Plate 10 1/4 x 13 3/4 in.; sheet 13 1/4 x 18 in.
Gift of Nellie and Art Werger, 2004

150. RICHARD SLOAT (born 1945)
Walk Down St. Mark's 1994
Etching and aquatint
Plate 11 7/8 x 17 7/8 in.; sheet 18 7/8 x 24 1/8 in.
Gift of the artist, 2004

151. ART WERGER (born 1955)
Daybreak 1997
Mezzotint
Plate 10 1/2 x 13 3/4 in.; sheet 15 5/8 x 20 1/4 in.
Gift of Nellie and Art Werger, 2004

152. DANIEL HAUBEN (born 1956)
Evening Rain 1998
Color intaglio
Plate 15 7/8 x 19 7/8 in.; sheet 22 3/8 x 26 1/4 in.
Purchase, 2003

153. BILL MURPHY (born 1952)
From Silver Lake 1999
Etching
Plate: 11 x 16 in.; sheet 12 1/4 x 17 1/2 in.
Gift of the artist, 2004

154. STEVEN WALKER (born 1955)
Sunset Skyline [View from the artist's studio in Astoria, Queens] 1997
Two-color aquatint (with surface roll)
Plate 7 1/4 x 9 5/8 in.; sheet 11 1/8 x 15 in.
Gift of the artist, 2004

155. EMILY TRUEBLOOD (born 1942)
World Trade View 1995
Two-color linocut
Image 8 x 6 in.; sheet 15 x 12 1/4 in.
Gift of the artist, 2004

156. SU-LI HUNG (American, born Taiwan, 1947; to New York 1970)
Broken City 2001
Color woodcut
Image 10 3/4 x 9 1/2 in.; sheet 15 3/4 x 15 7/8 in.
Gift of the artist, 2004

157. SU-LI HUNG (American, born Taiwan, 1947; to New York 1970)
World Trade Center 2001
Woodcut
Image 16 1/4 x 9 1/2 in.; sheet 20 x 15 in.
Gift of the artist, 2004

158. MARTIN LEVINE (born 1945)
42nd and 5th [View of New York Public Library] 1998
Etching and aquatint on chine collé
Image 4 3/8 x 7 7/16 in.; sheet 11 x 12 3/4 in.
Gift of the artists, 2004

159. MICHAEL DI CERBO (born 1947)
Parapets 2001
Etching and aquatint
Plate 5 3/4 x 7 7/8 in.; sheet 10 1/2 x 12 in.
Gift of the artist, 2004

160. RED GROOMS (born 1937)
On Your Mark, Get Set, Go! 2002
Color lithograph, published by Marlborough Graphics
Image 30 x 22 1/2 in.; sheet 35 x 26 3/8 in.
Purchase, Henry Luce Fund, 2004

161. KAREN WHITMAN (born 1953)
Downtown 2003
Linocut
Image 31 1/2 x 18 in.; sheet 39 x 23 7/8 in.
Gift of the artist, 2004

162. MICHAEL PELLETTIERI (born 1943)
City Signs [Brooklyn-Queens Expressway] 2003
Lithograph
Image 12 x 17 3/4 in.; sheet 14 13/16 x 22 1/8 in.
Gift of the artist, 2004

163. PHYLLIS SELTZER (born 1928)
Intersection 1999–2000
Heat transfer print
Image 39 x 47 1/4 in.; sheet 42 x 51 1/8 in.
Gift of the artist, 2004

164. ART WERGER (born 1955)
Attraction (Times Square, New York) 2003
Mezzotint
Image 23 1/2 x 25 3/8 in.; sheet 27 1/2 x 39 1/16 in.
Gift of Nellie and Art Werger, 2004

165. YVONNE JACQUETTE (born 1934)
New York Harbor Composite 2003
Woodcut
Image 44 1/2 x 32 in.; sheet 44 3/4 x 32 3/4 in.
Purchase, Henry Luce Fund, and gift of the artist and Mary Ryan Gallery, 2004

SELECTED BIBLIOGRAPHY

Beall, Karen F. et al., with an introduction by Alan Fern and a foreword by Carl Zigrosser. *American Prints in the Library of Congress: A Catalogue of the Collection*. Baltimore and London: The Johns Hopkins Press for the Library of Congress, 1970.

Borne, Mortimer, with R. S. Biran, *Drypoints, Etchings, Color Drypoints*. New York: Abaris Books, 1980.

Bumgardner, Georgia Brady. "George and William Endicott, Commercial Lithography in New York, 1831-51." In *Prints and Printmakers of New York State, 1825–1940*. Ed. David Tatham. Syracuse, N.Y.: Syracuse University Press, 1986, 43–65.

Burns, Ric, and James Sanders, with Lisa Ades. *New York, An Illustrated History*. New York: Alfred A. Knopf, 2003.

Campbell, Scot A. *The Graphic Work of T. F. Simon*. Chicago: Frederick Baker, Inc., 2002.

Carbonell, John. "Anthony Imbert, New York's Pioneer Lithographer." In *Prints and Printmakers of New York State, 1825–1940*. Ed. David Tatham. Syracuse, N.Y.: Syracuse University Press, 1986, 11–41.

Cortissoz, Royal, and the Leonard Clayton Gallery. *Catalogue of the Etchings and Drypoints of Childe Hassam*. San Francisco: Alan Wofsy Fine Arts, 1989.

Davis, Elliot Bostwick. "The Currency of Culture: Prints in New York City." In *Art and the Empire City: New York, 1825–1861*. Ed. Catherine Hoover Voorsanger and John K. Howat. New York, New Haven, and London: The Metropolitan Museum of Art with Yale University Press, 2000, 188–225.

Deák, Gloria Gilda, with an introduction by James Thomas Flexner. *American Views, Prospects and Vistas*. New York: The Viking Press and the New York Public Library, 1976.

———. *Picturing America, 1497–1899: Prints, Maps, and Drawings Bearing on the New World Discoveries and on the Development of the Territory that is now the United States*. 2 vols. Princeton, N.J.: Princeton University Press, 1988.

———. *Picturing New York: The City from its Beginnings to the Present*. New York: Columbia University Press, 2000.

———. *William James Bennett, Master of the Aquatint View*. New York: New York Public Library, 1988.

Diamonstein, Barbaralee. *The Landmarks of New York*. Third edition. New York: Harry N. Abrams, Inc., 1998.

Dolkart, Andrew S. *Morningside Heights, A History of its Architecture and Development*. New York: Columbia University Press, 1998.

Faberman, Hilarie, et al. *Aerial Muse: The Art of Yvonne Jacquette, including a Catalogue Raisonné of Prints*. New York: Hudson Hills Press in association with the Iris and B. Gerald Cantor Center for Visual Arts at Stanford University, 2002.

Falk, Peter Hastings, ed. *Who Was Who in American Art, 1564–1975: 400 Years of Artists in America*. Madison, Conn.: Sound View Press, 1999.

Gale Research Company, compiler, with an introduction by Bernard F. Reilly. *Currier & Ives. A Catalogue Raisonné: A Comprehensive Catalogue of the Lithographs of Nathaniel Currier, James Merritt Ives, and Charles Currier, including Ephemera associated with the Firm, 1834–1907*, 2 vols. Detroit: Gale Research Co., 1984.

Gray, Christopher. *New York Streetscapes: Tales of Manhattan's Buildings and Landmarks*. New York: Harry N. Abrams, Inc., 2003.

Hallam, John. "The Eighteenth-Century American Townscape and the Face of Colonialism." *Smithsonian Studies in American Art* (Summer–Fall 1990): 145–62.

Hartley, Craig. *Darkness into Light: Craig McPherson and the Art of the Mezzotint*. Cambridge, England: The Fitzwilliam Museum, 1998.

Heckscher, Morrison H. "Building the Empire City: Architects and Architecture." In *Art and the Empire City: New York, 1825–1861*. Eds. Catherine Hoover Voorsanger and John K. Howat. New York, New Haven, and London: The Metropolitan Museum of Art with Yale University Press, 2000, 168–87.

Heilbrun, Margaret. "NYork, NCentury, N-YHS." *The New-York Journal of American History* (Spring 2003): 19–32.

Heilbrun, Margaret, ed., with an introduction by Hugh Hardy. *Inventing the Skyline: The Architecture of Cass Gilbert*. New York: Columbia University Press, 2000.

Hone, Philip. *Diaries*, 28 vols. (1826–51), manuscript. Collection of the New-York Historical Society Library.

Hone, Philip, with an introduction by Allan Venins, ed. *The Diary of Philip Hone, 1828–1851*. New York: Dodd, Meade, 1936.

Jackson, Kenneth T., ed. *The Encyclopedia of New York City*. New Haven and London: Yale University Press and The New-York Historical Society, 1995.

Koke, Richard J., ed. *American Landscape and Genre Paintings in The New-York Historical Society: A Catalog of the Collection, including Historical, Narrative, and Marine Art*. 3 vols. Boston: The New-York Historical Society in assoc. with G. K. Hall and Co., 1982.

Marzio, Peter C. *The Democratic Art: Pictures for a 19th-Century America: Chromolithography, 1840–1900*. Boston: David R. Godine, in association with the Amon Carter Museum of Western Art, 1979.

Mayor, A. Hyatt. *Prints and People: A Social History of Printed Pictures*. New York: The Metropolitan Museum of Art, 1971.

McCarron, Paul. *The Prints of Martin Lewis, A Catalogue Raisonné*. Bronxville, N.Y.: M. Hausberg, 1995.

Morse, Peter, with a foreword by Jacob Kainen. *John Sloan's Prints: A Catalogue Raisonné of the Etchings, Lithographs, and Posters*. New Haven: Yale University Press, 1969.

Mushabac, Jane, and Angela Wigan. *A Short and Remarkable History of New York City with Illustrations from the Museum of the City of New York*. New York: Fordham University Press, 1999

The New-York Historical Society. *Quarterly*, vols 1–64 (1917–80).

Ogura, Tadao, et al. *The Complete Woodblock Prints of Yoshida Hiroshi*. Tokyo: Abe Corporation, 1987.

Olds, Irving S. *Bits and Pieces of American History as told by a Collection of American Naval and other Historical Prints and Paintings....*New York: n.p., 1951.

Peters, Harry T. *Currier & Ives, Printmakers to the American People*. Garden City, N.Y.: Doubleday, Doran Co., Inc., 1942.

Placzek, Adolf K., ed. *Macmillan Encyclopedia of Architects*. 4 vols. New York: Free Press, and London: Collier Macmillan, 1982.

Reps, John W. *Views and Viewmakers of Urban America: Lithographs of Towns and Cities in the United States and Canada, Notes on the Artists and Publishers, and a Union Catalog of Their Work, 1825–1925*. Columbia: University of Missouri Press, 1984.

Reps, John W. *Bird's Eye Views: Historic Lithographs of North American Cities*. New York: Princeton Architectural Press, 1998.

Robinson, Susan Barnes, and John Pirog. *Mabel Dwight: A Catalogue Raisonné of the Lithographs*. Washington, D.C. and London: Smithsonian Institution Press, 1997.

Rose, Ingrid, and Ralph Jentsch, eds. *Werner Drewes: A Catalogue Raisonné of his Prints/ Werner Drewes: Das Graphische Werk*. Munich and New York: Verlag Kunstgalerie Esslingen, 1984.

Rub, Timothy F. "American Architectural Prints." *Print Review* 18 (1984): 7–19.

Schutz, Anton. *New York in Etchings*. New York: Bard Brothers, 1939.

Shadwell, Wendy J., with a preface by A. Hyatt Mayor, a foreword by Donald H. Karshan, and an introduction by J. William Middendorf II. *American Printmaking, the First 150 Years*. Washington, D.C.: Smithsonian Institution Press for the Museum of Graphic Art, 1969.

Shadwell, Wendy J. "Prized Prints: Rare American Prints before 1860 in the Collection of The New-York Historical Society." *Imprint* 11 (Spring 1986): 1–27.

Stern, Robert A. M., et al. *New York 1900: Metropolitan Architecture and Urbanism, 1890-1915*. New York: Rizzoli, 1983.

Stern, Robert A. M., Gregory Gilmartin, and Thomas Mellins. *New York 1930*. New York: Rizzoli. 1987.

Stokes, I. N. Phelps. *The Iconography of Manhattan Island, 1498-1909: Compiled from Original Sources and Illustrated by Photo-Intaglio Reproductions of Important Maps, Plans, Views, and Documents in Public and Private Collections*. 6 vols. New York: Robert H. Dodd, 1915–26.

Stokes, I. N. Phelps, and Daniel C. Haskell. *American Historical Prints: Early Views of American Cities, etc. from the Phelps Stokes and Other Collections*. New York: New York Public Library, 1933.

Sullivan, Larry E. "The Print Collections of The New-York Historical Society." *Imprint* 6 (Autumn 1981): 20–24.

Tatham, David, ed. *Prints and Printmakers of New York State, 1825–1940*. Syracuse, N.Y.: Syracuse University Press, 1986.

Trager, James. *The New York Chronology*. New York: Harper Resource, 2003.

Vail. R. W. G. *Knickerbocker Birthday: A Sesqui-centennial History of The New-York Historical Society, 1804–1954*. New York: The New-York Historical Society, 1954.

Wall, Jr., Alexander J. "The Great Fire of 1835." *The New-York Journal of American History* (Spring 2003): 33–38.

White, Norval, and Elliot Willensky. *AIA Guide to New York City*. Fourth edition. New York: Three Rivers Press, 2000.

Wuerth, Louis A., with an introduction by Elizabeth Robins Pennell. *Catalogue of the Etchings of Joseph Pennell*. Boston: Little, Brown, 1928.

Zinkham, Helena. *A Guide to Print, Photograph, Architecture & Ephemera Collections at The New-York Historical Society*. New York: The New-York Historical Society, 1998.

INDEX